Making the Right Moves: Rikers Island & NYC Corrections

Mike Pisano

Enjoy!

Roy
9-9-19

Making the Right Moves: Rikers Island & NYC Corrections

BEING CALM IN THE STORM

Roy J. Caldwood

Copyright © 2015 Roy J. Caldwood
All rights reserved.
ISBN: 1511439831
ISBN-13: 9781511439831
Library of Congress Control Number: 2015904778
CreateSpace Independent Publishing Platform
North Charleston, South Carolina

Dedication

This book is dedicated to the three most important people in my life: my wife, Muriel, and my two daughters, Karen and Diane. I also dedicate this book to the inmates who saved my life during the 1972 riot when I was taken hostage. I wish that I had been able to personally thank those inmates who saved my life and took the extra steps to safeguard me while I was being held hostage. I additionally want to recognize those brave correctional officers who carried out my tough commands during the 1975 riot and never once backed down from their duty. These men exemplified the utmost in bravery, courage, and dedication—even when their own lives were at risk.

Table Of Contents

Foreword— Reflections on Roy Caldwood
by Michael Gelb (Editor)··ix
Preface ···xv
Chapter 1— Hostage!·······································1
Chapter 2— Beginnings ····································13
Chapter 3— Hart Island and City Jail ······················23
Chapter 4— A Day in Jail·································33
Chapter 5— Overcrowding, Riots, and Other Hazards ······41
Chapter 6— Hostage No More·····························55
Chapter 7— Force and Violence ···························60
Chapter 8— Inmate Grievances: They Were Real··········66
Chapter 9— Jobs Can Help Keep the Peace ···············74
Chapter 10— The Trouble with Bail ·······················79
Chapter 11— Drugs······································85
Chapter 12— The Big Bear ·······························96
Chapter 13— A Good Officer: What It Takes···············104
Chapter 14— The Black Panthers and Other Tests·········114
Chapter 15— A Snitch and an Escape Stopped ············123
Chapter 16— In the Library ·······························127
Chapter 17— Weddings Let in Some Light ················132
Chapter 18— One More Riot ·····························143
Chapter 19— Time for Roy to Go ·························153
Chapter 20— In Conclusion ······························162

Acknowledgments · 173
Author Bio · 177
Special Tribute · 179

FOREWORD

Reflections on Roy Caldwood by Michael Gelb

I first met Roy Caldwood in October 2013, having been approached by a mutual acquaintance—a client of mine, a cousin to Roy—to help him tell the story of his life as a correctional officer (CO) at Rikers Island and other New York City jails. I knew nothing about the correctional officers who keep the jails running and barely distinguished them from the police. I had never thought about what happens to people between the time they are arrested for a crime and the time they stand trial. Nor did I realize that huge numbers are stuck in jail for months—sometimes years—before their cases are heard. At that time, I could not have told you the difference between a jail and a prison. In fact, I probably didn't realize there was any difference at all.

My impressions, to the extent I had any at all, had been formed by movies and TV. I knew the Bible-quoting but viciously manipulative warden of *The Shawshank Redemption*, the sadistic prison-farm supervisor of *Cool Hand Luke*, and the coldly brutal officers who beat prisoners in scores of films.

But Roy opened my eyes. The first surprise was the way he thinks about his job. I thought of correctional officers as guards (a word the COs don't use about themselves). Roy explains it differently. "The job of a correctional officer," he says, "is to protect inmates."

The more we talked, the more it became clear to me that after twenty-one years in the correctional system watching over murderers, rapists, and other criminals; struggling to control addicts and the mentally ill who were behind bars; and being taken hostage, Roy had assumed the role of a powerful and thoughtful caregiver. It was not what I had expected at all.

He wanted to give the inmates productive activities to get them through the day. He listened to their complaints and suggestions and responded positively when possible. He tried to instill self-discipline by requiring them to keep their cells and living spaces clean. He hoped good habits would stay with the prisoners after they left jail and help give them a better chance to make it on the outside. But he concedes that, as a rule, jail living is more likely to drive inmates deeper into criminality than to reform them. "There isn't much correction in jail," he laments.

At the bottom, his approach came down to one principle: treat inmates with respect. "They're human beings like you and me," he says.

Roy spent his career finding the right moves to help the inmates when he could and to make life in jail a bit better, instead of a bit worse. He said being a good CO takes the ability of a chess master who can see how each move affects the next. But it also requires fast and instinctive decisions that you can't always explain.

"I just went with my gut," he says.

Like anybody who goes against the grain, Roy has his admirers, but also his detractors.

Among the fans is Jackie McMickens, a correctional officer who later became the first black woman to become commissioner of New York City's Department of Correction. To McMickens, who says Roy became a legend within the department, Roy's gift was treating inmates "like men" and "nurturing the best instincts in people."

She also raves about what she calls "Royisms"—taking a risk and doing something different.

"He was a legend. He did what they called weird—in those days—weird things. He would bring inmates and give them jobs. There were no jobs. You just didn't bring inmates out of cellblocks and give them tasks to do. And nobody talked about it even though it was 'illegal.' He just did that," she explains.

Warden James Thomas, Roy's boss for most of his time at Rikers, was a fan, too.

Roy recalls Thomas fondly: "He trusted me. He let me try things."

Roy encountered others, probably the majority back then, who didn't see it his way. To many inside the system, prisoners were, and still are, a faceless herd worthy of little personal consideration. To Roy's doubters, an inmate's only "right" is to do as he's told, without question or without challenge. They see force as an effective way to maintain control. To some of them, Roy was a soft heart who cared too much about the inmates.

What I see isn't softness, but uncommon strength—especially the confidence to do what he believed was right even when others tried to push him the other way.

In his earliest days, Roy admits, he used the tough-guy approach and would even slap inmates to make a point—an approach he looks back on with regret. But as he gained experience, he blazed a new path. He came to see force as an absolute last resort—and even then, he used just enough of it to get the job done. Ron Taylor, a retired state correctional sergeant whom Roy mentored, said that instead of force, "Roy taught me that the most important tool that you have as an officer is your brain."

Roy preferred a nonviolent approach in the belief that results would be better and cooperation more likely if he talked to inmates like equals, listened to their problems and suggestions, and showed them that he cared. In McMickens's words, "Roy went around nurturing the best instincts in people."

Standing just about five feet seven, Roy spent his life looking up at others who were physically more commanding. But he has an air of toughness and confidence often missing from larger men. His fists were quick when they needed to be. Despite his preference for cooperation, he says he didn't back down if a fight was forced on him.

Roy's a black man pained by the growing number of African Americans in jail and disturbed that the system seems much tougher on people of color than on whites. But he refuses to be defined by race. He insists that during his career he received fair treatment from most of his superiors, and he worked hard to be color-blind when doing his job.

Roy is still fit and wiry at ninety-two, and his head is topped by a full complement of salt-and-pepper hair. His eyes still light up with excitement as he shares his stories, which are spiced with insights on the correctional system. He pulses with the energy of a much younger man, and his intensity is almost visible. His passion for fairness and justice remains strong, but he's not interested in excusing criminals. As a husband, father, and great-grandfather, he wants safe streets for his family. But he distinguishes between dangerous, irreconcilable criminals and the struggling poor, the addicts, and the mentally ill who make up the bulk of the jail population—often for petty offenses.

"Nobody should be in jail because they're poor," he says. He's angry that too many people wind up behind bars because they lack the cash to post bail or pay the fines that come with low-level crimes and misdemeanors.

He wants America to do a better job of finding the right consequences for people who break the law. To Roy, long prison terms make sense as punishment for violent criminals and career lawbreakers who knowingly and routinely brush aside the law. But he insists that the justice system should focus on helping inmates repair their lives instead of warehousing them behind bars. His approach would require more money and energy for rehabilitation, mental health treatment, training programs, and other non-jail alternatives that help lesser "criminals" stay on the right side of the law. But he notes that locking people up costs large sums too, and that four years in a state university is less expensive than a year in a New York City jail.

He bristles at the case of Eric Garner, a New York City man who died in a police chokehold for illegally peddling a pack of cigarettes. "Cigarettes," Roy says, shuddering with dismay. "You don't kill a man for cigarettes." He is disgusted that a homeless man arrested for sleeping under a staircase died in an overheated cell at Rikers Island because correctional officers ignored how hot it was.

The stop-and-frisk policies that outraged civil libertarians but that defenders say have sharply cut crime in New York are a source of nuanced outrage to Roy. "Some neighborhoods need stop-and-frisk. There is way too much crime. But first build community support. Let them know what you are doing and why. Otherwise, it comes across as oppression." He adds that there are right ways and wrong ways to do a search: "Treat them with respect. You don't have to humiliate people, too." As a CO, Roy made his own path with innovations and experiments that others didn't dare. This book tells that story in Roy's words and through Roy's eyes.

If you want to get to know Roy Caldwood and gain a glimpse into his world, turn the pages.

Preface

This book is the story of my experience in New York City's jails. My name is Roy Caldwood, and I was a correctional officer (CO), not a prisoner. During my twenty-one years in that world, I was alternatively an authority figure, a confessor, a sympathetic ear, a mean SOB, a wedding planner, an entertainment director, an inmate advocate, a captor, and a hostage. And, in the end, I believe that I became prey.

I wrote this book to share my insights about what goes on inside prisons and jails. I hope that my story, the things I saw, and the lessons I learned will encourage others to reconsider the purpose of the prison system, to acknowledge inmates' humanity, and to think hard about how we might change the system to achieve better results both for the prisoners and for ourselves.

I worked in four institutions, but spent most of my time at two of them: the Manhattan Detention Complex, popularly known as the Tombs, and Rikers Island, where I spent the final fourteen years of my career. For the most part, these facilities served as detention centers, or "jails," where prisoners were held while awaiting trial or sentencing after a conviction. Rikers was a penitentiary, or "prison," for convicted criminals when I arrived there, but it was later converted to a detention center.[1]

---

1 As a rule, a detention center holds prisoners while they await trial and/or sentencing and is referred to as a "jail." A penitentiary or "prison" is an institution for inmates who have been convicted and sentenced to serve a year or more. Because most of my career

I ended my career as an assistant deputy warden at Rikers, where I also served as the program director for all programs within my institution. In that role, I provided inmates with recreational and educational options, including an arts program and a basketball league. I brought in music, stage performances, other live entertainment, and eventually even a rodeo. I worked with dedicated volunteers who tried to give prisoners the tools to succeed as law-abiding citizens once they left jail. I also worked with drug addicts, a difficult and frustrating assignment that helped convince me that we need a smarter approach to illegal drugs. **Late in my career I was taken hostage, but that didn't mute my joy when I was able to help inmates or arrange weddings so they could get married while living behind bars.**

I have been out of that life for many years, and no doubt there have been changes during my retirement. For one, the US prison population has more than quintupled over that time. Mandatory minimum sentencing and three-strike statutes, which were enacted during the "law-and-order" crackdown of the late 1960s and early 1970s, have made the United States the world's leading jailer. Rikers Island, which housed perhaps three thousand inmates[2] in three facilities when I started there, is now "home" to more than twelve thousand prisoners in ten separate facilities.

The population of inmates has shifted from mostly white when I started my career to heavily black and Hispanic today. Some of that reflects population change within the boundaries of New York City because so many whites have left for the suburbs. But there's no doubt that the justice

---

was spent in detention centers, I have generally used the term "jail" except for specific situations where "prison" is the technically correct term.

2   When I refer to inmates and prisoners throughout this book I use masculine pronouns and the word "men" because I worked exclusively with male inmates during my career. At that time, men's institutions were staffed exclusively by men COs and women's institutions were staffed by women COs. It is also worth noting that men account for more than 90 percent of inmates in jails and prisons today.

system is tougher on people of color. This book is not about the problems of race, but as a black man I cannot ignore that obvious fact.

Drug-related offenses, relatively rare when I began working as a CO, became increasingly common in the latter stages of my career and exploded after I retired. Today, using, possessing, buying, or selling drugs puts more people behind bars than any other offense—a trend that made my work much tougher and that I believe raises important questions about whom we put in jail and why. As I write, there is an emerging movement, which I support, to revise these laws, reduce the number of people locked up for drug offenses, and divert more drug offenders to treatment programs.

Tragically, a number of recent investigations suggest that Rikers Island is now a place where many COs treat inmates with systematic brutality. Rikers was always a hard place to be, but the sort of violence that these reports suggest takes place today did not exist during my career. Prisoners' complaints back then focused more on the conditions of daily living: overcrowding, poor medical care, communications with family, visitation rules, bad food, boredom, and poor facilities. Yes, some COs hit prisoners, but there were clear lines that were rarely crossed. The concerted, planned beatings and brutality we hear about today are a new phenomenon.

Despite these changes, I believe my story remains relevant and can give people a better sense of what happens inside our country's jails. To the extent caricatures have taken hold or popular entertainment has provided a distorted picture, I offer this book as a more accurate picture for those who have never set foot in a penal institution.

Some things about incarceration are constant. Most fundamentally, penal institutions are a bad place to spend time, and that is true for COs and inmates alike. Most obviously, prisoners lose their freedom. Even in the best of circumstances, losing the ability to control how one spends his or her time is a painful and humbling experience. Prisoners are told when to eat, what to eat, what work they can and cannot do, when to sleep and when to wake up, and when they can have a visitor.

One man's story can never provide the whole truth about something as large as the US correctional system, which houses about 2.3 million inmates. Each of the institutions I served in had its own personality. Each jail or prison has its own purpose, its own patterns, and its unique mixture of inmates, correctional officers, and wardens.

Writing this book has been an exercise in self-discovery. I realized that I had developed a philosophy about my job and how to treat the inmates that I was empowered to oversee. The way I interacted with prisoners evolved as I learned the jail environment. **I came to think of myself as a caregiver who tried to keep the institution running more smoothly, in part by listening to what the prisoners had to say.** As I reflected and took this look backward, I identified some realities of life in jail.

Reality Number One—Inmates are human beings.

With COs on one side of an unequal relationship and inmates on the other, a jail or prison is a collection of individuals with varying talents, moods, and needs. Prisoners and COs must learn workable ways to get through the day in relative peace. They have to find some type of balance to their interactions so that COs can exercise the necessary level of authority in a way that gives the inmates basic human respect.

That doesn't mean inmates and officers should be friends or even like each other. But it means that **whatever their crimes, inmates are entitled to a basic level of respect and dignity.** Listening to what they say can make the institution run better and, perhaps, help prisoners strengthen the better parts of their nature. Often, inmates have legitimate grievances: bad food, poor medical care, harassment by other inmates or COs, or a cellmate who makes it difficult to get along. Those sorts of complaints should be addressed and corrected if possible.

Early in my career, I was counseled, "Don't talk to them; give orders." Fraternizing was frowned upon. But I never could fully follow those instructions. Instead, I listened. I asked prisoners for suggestions when they had a complaint, and I thought hard about how to make conditions better. In this way, I went against the grain. When their ideas made sense, I would talk to the warden and see what was possible. Those conversations were the root of a prison arts program, midnight basketball, and other inmate activities I eventually brought to Rikers Island.

Activities for inmates also make the officers' lives a bit easier, too. I believed the inmates would be more peaceful, more cooperative, and better able to survive in prison if we gave them things to do. The more time on their hands and the more bored they might be, the more likely they were to cause trouble, if only to make the time pass.

Unfortunately, bad things happen in prison. Just as on the outside, the strong prey on the weak. Physical abuse and sexual assaults occur. Sadly, we can't always keep prisoners safe from each other or from abusive officers.

R<small>EALITY</small> N<small>UMBER</small> T<small>WO</small>—T<small>OO MANY</small> A<small>MERICANS ARE BEHIND BARS.</small>

Our country puts people in jail or prison at a higher rate than any other country in the world, quite often for reasons that don't make sense. If you are imprisoned in America, there's a pretty good chance you are poor, mentally ill, addicted to drugs, or an alcoholic. You probably have relatively little education, and it's likely that you are black or Hispanic. In addition to those who have committed major crimes, jail inmates also include homeless people arrested for sleeping in parks or stairwells, poor people who can't pay traffic fines, and people who've partied too long and too hard and disturbed the peace or peed behind a bush.

Putting violent offenders and career criminals in prison is OK by me. Some people are too dangerous to walk freely; sometimes, punishment is reasonable for its own sake. But I believe we should think harder about which of the lesser offenders belong in a correctional institute and which should be placed in some type of alternative—drug rehab, a mental health treatment program, supervised release, job training, or even community service.

Locking up so many people overcrowds the jails, and it is a big reason for the abuses that take place in some correctional institutions. Often, there are more inmates than the jail was built for and too few correctional officers to keep control while also giving prisoners the care they should have.

Reality Number Three—There's not enough correction in jail.

Despite its hopeful name, the Department of Corrections does not do much corrections work. Time in jail is something of a trade meeting for criminals, a place where they can share information about how to commit crimes more effectively. Jail is more likely to help inmates perfect their criminal skills than it is to reform them.

Spending time in jail generally makes it even harder to succeed legally, and many inmates break the law again soon after they are released. Even when prisoners are extremely motivated, it's hard for them to stay straight after they are freed. As Jennifer Wynn explains in her excellent book *Inside Rikers*,³ they go back to the same neighborhoods and the same temptations. Jobs are hard to come by, and the pay usually isn't very good. Employers are reluctant to hire ex-cons, and landlords are skeptical of them, too. In that situation, an "easy score" is hard for many former inmates to resist.

Corrections officials recognize the need for rehab, education, and training programs, but they usually lack the resources. Some private citizens and organizations try to fill the void by helping inmates develop the skills and confidence to build new lives. But most former prisoners are running uphill, and it wasn't really a surprise to see the same faces coming back again and again to Rikers. Our country doesn't do enough to help them along either while they're locked up or after they're released.

REALITY NUMBER FOUR—THE BEST DAY INSIDE A JAIL IS STILL A BAD DAY.

Penal institutions are snake pits of inmates of varying personalities, sizes, shapes, and colors who take part in shifting alliances and dangerous competition. Danger can sizzle and strike without warning and from almost any spot as inmates compete for dominance, power, sex, drugs, food, and weapons. Prisoners jockey for advantage, and COs seek ways to maintain control while dealing with a haphazard collection of inmates who behave in unpredictable ways.

COs are vulnerable. They are significantly outnumbered at all times. At Rikers, when I was there, a single officer might be responsible for 150 inmates walking without restrains within a cellblock. As a matter of course, officers are unarmed. But they are expected to control a population that breaks laws, ignores rules, and may wish to hurt them. Even in

---

3 Jennifer Wynn, *Inside Rikers: Stories from the World's Largest Penal Colony* (New York: St. Martin's Griffin, 2001).

the best-run institutions, inmates can often get a weapon smuggled in from outside or craft one from the ordinary items they find in jail. The environment wears you down. For me, the day's best moment was stepping outside to go home.

Reality Number Five—COs can generally maintain control without using violence.

COs have the law and the institution on their side. Regrettably, it took me a long time on the job to recognize this. In my early years on the job, I thought a sudden slap to the face was an effective tool.

As I was on the job longer, my methods evolved. I learned better what works and what doesn't, and I became a more effective correctional officer Acting with confidence was self-fulfilling. Letting prisoners see that I was in charge made it so. Showing firmness when necessary created credibility that worked to my advantage. But showing that I cared about the inmates was important as well. Maintaining control is far easier if the system effectively addresses prisoners' legitimate grievances.

Well-run institutions and smart COs look for positive incentives. But the fear of consequences also encourages prisoners to cooperate. If a prisoner acts out, he can lose privileges. More negatively, prisoners know that undue defiance or assaulting an officer could have severe consequences. And, to be honest, prisoners worry about being beaten. It's not supposed to happen, and it shouldn't, but sometimes it does, and inmates know it's possible.

Reality Number Six—No matter how hard I tried, I couldn't always keep trouble out of jail.

Prisoners often abuse one another. Rapes, assaults, and intimidation go on in prison. No matter how hard COs work to prevent trouble, the crimes that take place on the outside happen inside as well. Drugs and weapons can almost always be smuggled in.

In my career, I was taken hostage. I survived a prison riot. In my final year as an ADW, I became prey for some prisoners who believed they could hurt me with impunity. I sensed that the arrival of a new warden had stripped me of basic support and put my life at risk. Perhaps after twenty-one years I was just worn out, tired of the stresses, and seeing danger where I hadn't noticed it before. But that feeling of anxiety and dread told me it was time to move on.

So I walked out and didn't look back—until now, when I decided to put it down in this book.

I've come to believe our prison system doesn't keep us safe, at least not in the long run. Just as I couldn't keep trouble out of jail, prisons don't keep trouble out of society. Putting truly dangerous people in prison makes sense. But for most inmates, jail is a temporary holding place before we release them back into the world—without the needed repair work to give them a better chance. Many inmates come out of jail more damaged and dangerous than when they went in.

I'm not a criminologist. I don't have a PhD. But considering the number of people we lock up and the billions we spend to feed and house them, I know we aren't getting very good results. We need to find alternatives—rehab programs, education and training, monitored release-and-work programs, and community-based rehabilitation, to name a few. We need to find ways to strengthen inmates' community connections and the support systems that help them go straight. Most of the time, jail does the opposite.

These ideas aren't original with me. I can't say for certain which ones will work best, but I am sure that with a little ingenuity, we can do better. I am even surer that we must.

CHAPTER 1

Hostage!

I should have stayed in bed.

Sunday, February 27, 1972: a day off with the family. It was cold but sunny, the temperature right around freezing. Good weather for that time of year in New York. Then a ringing phone broke my relaxation. It was Deputy Warden Harris,[4] with "a small problem."

I knew better. I could count on one hand the number of times I'd been called at home for a small problem, and I didn't even need all five fingers to finish. As he talked, my gut instinct was confirmed. It was a big problem: Cuba was going to be transferred to the Tombs because his hearing date was coming up and the courthouse was right next door. To administrators, it's just standard procedure. But Cuba was the prisoners' leader in cellblock seven, and that meant hundreds of angry inmates who would see the transfer as retribution, a way for authorities at Rikers to get rid of the guy behind a riot we'd had just four weeks before.

---

4 With a single exception, I have changed the names of all correctional officers, inmates, wardens, and deputy wardens cited in this book. I do not know the whereabouts of these individuals, and many of them are likely deceased and would not have the opportunity to provide their perspectives of my accounts. I have identified Warden James Thomas by his real name as a lasting honor to his memory. I consider Warden Thomas one of the finest correctional officials I have ever known. I also have used the real names of public officials, including Commissioner Anna Kross, Judge Morris Lasker, District Attorney Burton Roberts, and Commissioner Bernard Malcolm.

The young inmates in block seven (who were between eighteen and twenty years old) were still seething over unresolved grievances, and they weren't feeling good about backing down earlier in the month. Locked in the adolescent house, they were full of testosterone and looking for a chance to show how they felt. They weren't going to like this news, and it could be just the excuse they needed for another insurrection.

So, it was a big problem. And it didn't have to be mine. I could have told the deputy, "I'm staying home." But some combination of pride and duty wouldn't let me say no. Bottom line: it was my job.

The bosses were looking to me for help. That was partly a reflection of my new status. Warden Thomas had always had my back and supported ideas of mine that Deputy Harris and others often thought were too sympathetic to the prisoners. They'd thought I was soft.

Their perceptions had changed a bit after I'd managed to defuse the uprising on February 1. Stopping the ruckus four weeks before was possible only because I was respected by Cuba and many of the other inmates. Officers who'd been skeptical of the way I went about my job had seen that treating people with basic respect could return benefits even in a prison. That "success" hadn't changed the way I approached my job or treated the prisoners. It was the way I'd always done things. But in some others' eyes, the world looked a bit different now.

I put got dressed, hugged my wife and my daughters, and pointed my car toward Rikers— one of the rottenest days of my life. To use a cliché, I went from sunlight into darkness. Nobody walks into a prison whistling a happy tune or thinking it's going to be a cheery day. But on this Sunday, I came much too close to never coming home again.

Before hanging up the phone, I'd told the deputy, "It's a big problem. I need a big force."

But when I got there, I had five officers in reserve for emergency response. In other words, I had nothing. Five officers on duty in the cellblock and five more in reserve—to face down as many as three hundred inmates if they decided to fight. What could I do with five men? I was the messenger with bad news for Cuba. The bosses had started a fire and were sending me with the gasoline. **Their thinking (hope?) was that Cuba wouldn't hurt someone he trusted. That someone was me. That's how I became a hostage.**

Cuba wasn't going to be happy with my news. His given name was Orlando, and he was proud of his Cuban heritage. His family had fled that country to get away from Fidel Castro's dictatorship. Even in jail, Orlando honored his native land and wanted to wave the Cuban flag on the country's national heritage day. So, he became "Cuba" to all who knew him inside. He had a bearing and sense of command. He was quick with his decisions, which he made decisively on his own without consultations with the other prisoners or any hem or haw about whether they'd follow him or not. I'd found he could typically deliver what he promised.

He'd found a niche at Rikers. On the street, he'd been just another young hustler. Inside, he'd become a leader. Going to the Tombs would have meant starting over. Like the popular kid whose parents told him that he had to go to a new school, why would he want to change?

And just because I got along with him wasn't going to change how he felt or what he would do about it. I was his jailer, not his friend. Neither one of us was ever confused about that.

After getting briefed in, I walked to block seven, where the tour commander and I called for Cuba. The three of us went to the officers' mess hall and we explained to Cuba that he was going to be moved. He reacted as I expected: "I'm not going, not going." He didn't want to be split up from his "crimey"—the buddy who'd been charged with him. He was concerned that a separation would put pressure on them to rat each other out. And he wanted his brother—also at Rikers—to go with him as well.

I told him I'd see what I could do but that one way or the other, he would be moved. "You can holler, scream, or fight," I said. "A whole bunch of guys will stand with you. But they will get hurt, and you *will* lose. One way or the other, peacefully or not, you are going to go."

He seemed to soften. He said if we could move his crimey and his brother with him, he would go. No fuss. No fight. We sent him back to his cell to get his things together. And I went into the block to wait.

The block held about 240 cells stacked in three tiers. In 1972, we had about 320 inmates there. Though built for one person, a lot of the cells were, in fact, housing two. Overcrowding was among the inmates' grievances, a source of tension that made my job harder every day of the week.

Cuba was up on the third tier. Except for six or seven inmates on the "house gang" who had been let out to clean up the area, the block was on lock-in. That was typical at that time of day, so I paid it no mind. The house gang was just background noise, almost invisible to my senses. That was my first mistake.

I sent word up to Cuba that it was time to go. In the past, he'd usually been pretty fast when I summoned. Nowhere to be seen, and then, *here*, next to me, ready to talk. So, I waited on tier one, "the flat," visible from above. Two minutes, three minutes, five minutes. No Cuba. There must have been a hang-up, some problem that the officer on duty couldn't set right. "Not good, not good," I said to myself.

Perhaps this was a moment when I might have turned around, gone back to the deputy, and considered another strategy or asked for a bigger force. But I didn't want to overreact. In hindsight, I also fell victim to habit: we were always short of resources and were used to making do. This was just one more time when I would have to make do.

I wanted to project business as usual, so I ignored the inmates shouting at me, "No, no captain; don't go, Cuba." I had my job, and I was going to do it. Head up, confident (or so I hoped it appeared), I strode to the end of the cellblock, a football-field-length walk, and walked up the steps to tier three. My mood was sour, my patience short, my anxiety rising. I barked, "Shut up," to a Hispanic inmate who was jabbering at me. He was a chronic complainer whom I knew better than I cared to. Every day, he had another problem. Typically, I'd hear him out. But this day, I had no patience for him. My annoyance was obvious.

Even before I got to Cuba's cell, a house gang member told me, "Cuba's not going." Cuba had changed his mind—or perhaps he'd lied to me all along to gain the space he needed to set off his rebellion.

Then, face to face, Cuba made his position clear. "I'm not going," he said. No drama, no threats, just a few words—straightforward as he'd always been.

I shook my head and told him that was a mistake. Knowing that his answer meant trouble, I turned to leave, explaining I would report our talk to the warden. At least that was my plan until Cuba told me his.

"You're not going anywhere," he said. Then, with some silent signal, the cellblock came alive. Somehow, the house gang had gotten the key to the panel box that controlled the cells. "Open the cells," he ordered, and in a moment, it was done.

Then I was grabbed. Inmates, including Cuba, had my arms and my shoulders. There were too many. They were young, strong, and bigger than me. Surprised and outnumbered, I couldn't fight them off.

The cells were open, the inmates were out, and I was about to go in. "Get in there," Cuba ordered with a nod to the closest cell. Then a shove, and I was in.

Pandemonium. On fire with energy, the inmates tore at their belongings, carting out bed frames, mattresses, toilet seats and tops, and chairs to build barricades at the cellblock gates. At the gate, they piled it all high, constructing a mountain of prison bric-a-brac and debris. A scaffold used for cleaning the cellblock became the centerpiece of the barricade. The scaffold blocked the gate and gave the prisoners a place to stand, to be up high, ready to swing down on any attacker below.

The barricade kept growing higher -- four feet, five feet, and more, designed to keep out the force of officers that would inevitably come to get me and also rescue the other officers who'd been taken captive while patrolling the block.

"No, Cuba, no. You've got the block; I can't stop you. No reason I need to be in a damn cell," I pleaded. "Let me talk to the warden." Cuba kept me in the cell. His fellows pulled off my shirt, confiscated my hat, and left me standing in my pants and a T-shirt. My badge, the symbol of authority, had been taken away.

Briefly panicked, I climbed up on the cell gate, gripping tight. "Don't lock it. Don't lock it. Leave it open!"

And Cuba locked the gate. "You'll be safer with it locked," he assured me. He was right. Left unlocked, any inmate could come in and try to hurt me or kill me. Just one enemy out of three hundred inmates, one moment amid chaos, and I could be dead. There was one more thing Cuba made sure I understood: "If they try to rescue you, I will kill you."

I couldn't breathe. I felt suffocated. Powerless. The ceiling seemed to be coming down on me, the walls closing in. **I was the captive. For the first time, I suppose, I felt what the inmates experienced every day.**

Adding salt to my wound, the Hispanic inmate I'd just yelled at was outside my cell—of all the inmates who might be out there. Now I was *his* prisoner. *You stupid son of a gun, Roy, you blew it. It's payback time,* I thought. But he was kind, solicitous. "They shouldn't lock you up," he said. "I'm going to tell them to let you out."

That's what I'd been begging for moments earlier. But now I'd pulled myself together. Cuba was right. I was safer locked up. "Hell, no. Leave it locked. Don't open the gate," I shouted back.

The inmate offered me his jacket, sewed for him by his mother. It was freezing outside and chilly in my cell, so a jacket might be nice. But, damn, then I'd really look like an inmate. When the warden sent a rescue team—and he would want to retake the block—there would be fighting, confusion, tumult, and crazy swinging at whoever moved. Looking like an inmate could be dangerous. I thanked him for the offer but shook my head no.

But I gladly took a towel. "Wet it when the tear gas comes in," he explained. "Wrap it on your face to cover your eyes."

Then, another offer I couldn't refuse—a cigarette. I didn't smoke, but I took his whole damn pack. I felt this would help me to keep a good rapport with him. When another inmate, standing with him, asked me to give him a cigarette, I said " hell no", and refused to give him one. I was testing the waters. I felt assured when I saw that he didn't just come in and take the cigarettes.

On edge, muscles taut, sweating. I fought to keep my mind sharp for good decision making. I had three other officers to worry about; I assumed they were all captive by now, too.

The inmates were giddy with their new freedom and power. Though still in a jail, the cellblock had become their turf. Outside my cell, they were celebratory and loud. And, taunting me, they were almost singing, "We're going to kill you, we're going to kill you." All they needed was a guitar. It was a taunt more than a real threat—or so I believed—but that positive spin didn't brighten my mood.

They knew a fight was likely coming, and they were building their barricade higher and tighter to the cellblock gate to keep the gate doors from opening inward when the officers decided to push their way into the block. The inmates had been locked up, bored and idle. They *wanted* to brawl, most of them, and they were ready. They were pumped; their adrenaline flowing—a mix of cockiness and fear that comes before the first blow.

I wanted to get my officers in one place if I could. I wanted to see their condition and reassure them—and myself—that things would work out OK. I asked to see Cuba. This time, he was Johnny-on-the-spot, materializing as if from thin air. Before, he'd made me wait, but now that he was in control, he moved fast.

I suggested to Cuba that he bring all the officers together where I could see them. It would be easier for me to plot out my moves if I could see where they were. And it would be easier for him to keep them safe against any crazy inmate who might decide to kill a CO when Cuba's eyes were elsewhere. That would mean a potential murder charge against every man in the block for creating danger, whether they'd raised their own hands against someone or not.

"Bring 'em here where I can help keep them calm," I pleaded with Cuba. "One wrong move, even a heart attack that kills an anxious officer, and you have a murder rap." In minutes, Cuba put us all together—one officer with me in my cell, and the three others in the cell next door. That calmed us all a bit because having a buddy nearby ended the isolation and eased the fear of being alone. A bit more at ease, I stretched out on the bed and put my head back to think, all the time telling myself, "I can't go to sleep. I need a clear head to be ready to act." Time was slow and heavy but strangely fast at the same time.

Suddenly, my brief calm was grabbed away. My cell door opened, and two inmates snatched me up. They hustled me out, all but dragging me down the stairs—one flight, then two, and then three floors down to the flat, where they flung me up onto a table and told me to stand in front of a window that faced the outside. The glass had been broken out, the better to show off their prize—me—to the officers gathering outside and standing below. I was on display.

"We've got Captain Caldwood. We've got Captain Caldwood," they chanted out through the shattered window. They were letting the warden know that I was alive but also at risk. To the prisoners, I was insurance, a possible get-out-of-jail-free card that might encourage negotiations—because as one inmate said: "The warden likes you. He doesn't want anything to happen to you."

That was the day's second miscalculation at my expense. The deputy thought because Cuba respected me, he might listen to me about his transfer, or at least he wouldn't hurt me. Cuba hoped the wardens' respect for me might make my personal safety the top priority so that the inmates could tear up the cellblock without penalty. Two wrong guesses. I suppose it was the price I paid for having the respect of both sides.

In fact, the warden and his superiors made a decision even before I was taken hostage: no negotiations. After the uprising at the start of the month, we'd been expecting a rerun at some point. But the next time, there wouldn't be deals or clemency. The inmates needed to be shown they didn't run the institution and that they couldn't disrupt the place, defy the rules, or go after officers and walk away without consequences.

Now, I was on display. Looking out, I saw the helmeted and jacketed force of COs gathering below. Their helmets were strapped, flak jackets buttoned, and riot batons clenched and ready to hurt a man badly. I raised my hand as if to say hello to the officers passing by. But if they recognized me, they didn't show it. My wave wouldn't change their plans. The battle for cellblock 7 was about to begin.

First came tear gas: acrid-smelling, eye-stinging vapor that can put a man to agony by swelling his eyes and burning his lungs. Perhaps the gas would kill the will to fight and persuade the prisoners to give up without blood, broken bones, and banged-up heads. At least that was the idea.

Looking out from the table, I saw an officer raising his big gun to fire the gas. It seemed centered dead on my head; I could be about to die. *Whup*, **the cannon shouted. A gas canister whizzed by my head. It rattled off the floor and exploded the gas into my eyes and up my nose.**

Then, more. A cacophony of canisters clanked off the walls, the cells, the bars and skittered across the floor. I was choking smoke blinded. Then I was yanked away again hustled back up the stairs, across the floor, and back into my cell. Dragged there, then here—none of it on my own. The inmates had a new taunt for me now: "They don't give a damn about you, Captain. They don't care if you die."

I was angry, frustrated, frightened. Trying to think how to end it, I called out, "Cuba, Cuba. We can stop this. We can fix this before it gets worse. I need to call the warden."

I really didn't know if I could do anything. But trying was better than waiting helplessly in my cell.

Then Cuba was there in front of me. He led me down to a small room near the front of the block. At the gate, I could study the barricades: the scaffold and mattresses piled high, the debris up against the gate to absorb an assault.

By the gate, Cuba escorted me to a little "office," really just an odd semienclosed cubicle with two walls of steel and two open sides. It wasn't much more than a place where an officer would usually sit. But there was a phone that connected to the control room. I hoped I would lift the phone on my end and the warden would answer on the other—and I could tell him to stop this.

Water was coming in now. The COs had big fire hoses, and they were working us over, trying to flood out the inmates. More tear gas, too.

I gripped the phone tightly to my face, my hands cupped around the mouthpiece so I'd be easier to hear, but I couldn't get through. Nobody was picking up on the other side. My cubicle felt like ground zero, with gas canisters flying to my left and to my right and over my head. If one hit me, I could die. It would hurt like hell, that was for sure.

My eyes on fire and clouded with smoke, I couldn't see. I was just this side of desperate, and no one would pick up the damn phone! I needed to talk to the warden. I was scrambling to head off the battle, but no one would take my call.

Then an inmate's voice pierced the chaos, pleading, "Come out. Come on out, Captain Caldwood. They're going to kill you." Then he grabbed my arm gently and led me out. I swear he saved my life. An inmate saved my life. I couldn't see who the young man was, and to this day I still don't know.

The next I knew, I was back in my cell. I don't remember how, but my anonymous savior had put me back there. Inmates were continuously walking passed our cells and shouting "we are going to kill you". This time they added additional words to their threats. "**We are going to kill you right now, starting here**".

All of our cells were opened and inmates went into **the cell next to me. I jumped up off of my bed in time to see two of my officers being brought out of their cell. They had hangman nooses, made from bed sheets, around their necks. I charged out of** my cell and called loudly for Cuba. " I want to see Cuba". Within seconds Cuba appeared. I told Cuba, if he killed any one of us, the penalty would be the same as if he killed the three of us. I let him know that my officers would then come in and kill every inmate in this cell block. Cuba then ordered that the nooses be removed from my officer's necks and had them returned to their cell.

CHAPTER 2

Beginnings

Of course, I wasn't always a hostage, or even a CO. Let me tell you how I got there.

I was born in 1922, at a hospital in Manhattan. But home was Harlem—in a fifth-floor walk-up on 153rd Street. It had three bedrooms, a living room, a dining room, a kitchen, and a bathroom. I lived there till I received my "greetings" draft letter from Uncle Sam and left for the army in 1943. That was the first time I'd live anywhere besides New York City, and the last time as well.

People forget, but back then Harlem was mostly white. Not that living amid a white majority affected my daily life much. Our block, our neighborhood, was black, like me—not by law, perhaps, but because neighborhoods were generally segregated in those days. The separation wasn't just by color, but by nationality or ethnicity. Black with Black. Irish with Irish. Jew with Jew. When people arrived in New York from some distant place, they looked for something familiar and comfortable. That often meant living near family or friends they had known before. Of course, most ethnic groups had a choice about where to live—but not black people. If you were black, there were only some parts of town where you could rent or buy a place to live. Segregation was a way of life.

The building where I grew up is long gone. It's just as well, because the Harlem of my youth is long gone, too, and I don't go back often to visit. In my day, families were mostly intact. Neighbors knew each other and looked out for one another. They took responsibility for each other's kids. That was good for us children, though at the time it just seemed like one more chance to be yelled at if we did something wrong. There were adult eyes all around, and that made us feel safe—if watched—in our small world.

At home, I was loved by two parents for a while, and then intensely and deeply by my mother after she and my father split apart. My father didn't disappear. We always knew where he lived. He stayed in touch and provided money when he could, and we stayed a connected father and son throughout his life.

Later, when I was a correctional officer in New York City prisons, many of the prisoners I watched over also were black men from Harlem. But in other ways, we came from different planets. People ask if I ever looked through the bars and saw myself looking back. Did I empathize, thinking, *That could be me?* I never did. I had human sympathy. We shared the bond of discrimination. But the connection was less than what some might imagine. We just weren't that much alike.

Different childhood experiences led us on our very different paths to prison and at least partly explain why I was on one side of the bars and they were on the other. I don't mean that our destinies were predetermined. But because of the way I was raised and the foundation it gave me, it was easier for me to make the right moves.

Let me tell you what my life was like.

We were poor. Very poor. My dad always had a job—he ran an elevator and drove a truck for a time. Five days a week, he showed me that work was the way to make your way. He always wore a suit, tie, and hat—men dressed more formally back then—and he carried himself with pride and dignity. In that way, he was a role model. I gave up the suit, but I've always tried to hang on to his bearing and his independence.

But there were limits to what types of jobs a black man could get, and my dad never could make very much money. Mom worked, too, operating office-building switchboards. We scraped by, but it was hard. There were five mouths to feed: Mom and Dad (till he left); me; my older sister, Marjorie; and my cousin Belle, who came to live with us when she was about ten.

Taking in my cousin was typical of my mother. Throughout her life, whether she had a lot or a little, she had an open-door policy: if you needed help, you could come in and get a meal. Helping each other was the way she thought we should live our lives.

When my parents split, money got even tougher to come by. My dad didn't smoke or drink, but he liked to play poker, and it began to dominate his weekends. Gambling wasn't unusual in Harlem. In fact, just about everybody played the numbers, laying out a nickel or dime and dreaming of hitting the big score. To my mother, that was foolishness, maybe even sinful. She couldn't make peace with my dad playing cards. Eventually, it drove them apart.

Crime was not a big problem in my neighborhood. As kids, we'd have our scrapes; we'd put up our dukes and wail away until we got tired or somebody said, "Give." No knives, no guns, not even sticks. I wasn't always the bravest in those battles. When I was very young, I would run home and get my cousin Belle for help when challenged. Finally, one of the older kids decided it was time I learned to stand on my own. He took me aside for some boxing lessons and gave me the confidence to fight my own battles.

I wasn't the biggest kid, but I was feisty and fearless—a bit foolish, too, I suppose—always ready to prove with my fists that I was right and you were wrong.

We didn't mess with drugs. If somebody wanted to feel a little high, booze was the way to go. Prohibition was the law, but it didn't seem to stop many people from drinking. Bootleg whiskey and the private "clubs" that sold it probably thought Prohibition was a great thing. It was the first example, for me, of a dumb law that didn't work out the way it was planned. All it did was create opportunity for lawbreakers. Later, **when I worked in the prison system, poorly conceived laws complicated my job by overcrowding the jails with people who probably didn't need to be there.**

None of this affected me directly, though, when I was growing up. I was just eleven when Prohibition was repealed. Not that it would have made a difference if I'd been older. Because of the way I was raised—a quick backhand slap from my mother or a hit with a ruler from the nuns at school if I did wrong—I didn't even think about breaking the law.

As a youngster, my only contact with the police was during stickball—not cops showing the kids how to play, but cops breaking up our games.

We played in the streets with a broomstick or a similar skinny bat and a pink rubber Spalding ball—a "Spal-DEEN," as we called it. Stickball was our big-time summer recreation. We'd play right in front of our homes with our parents watching from the front stoop or out the window.

But for some reason, the cops didn't like stickball, or at least they didn't like for us to play it. Running from the police was almost as much a part of the game as hitting the ball. For some reason that I can't figure out to this day, stickball set the cops whooping and hollering and racing at us with billy clubs swinging. For us kids, it was one eye on the ball and one eye out for the police, always ready to drop the stick, run, and taunt as we ran, "Brass buttons and blue coat can't catch a nanny goat." We didn't know what would happen if they caught us, but they never did. Looking back, maybe they never really wanted to catch us. Perhaps they just needed a little something to break the boredom of their day.

I went to Resurrection Elementary Parochial School, a Catholic school. The rules were strict, and the nuns could be tough; they had no qualms about scaring the children or smacking us. Once, in my first days at the school, I got out of hand, or at least my teacher thought so. She ordered two of the bigger kids to open the dumbwaiter door, pick me up, put me partway into the shaft in the wall, and threaten to dump me down if I didn't behave. I suppose the sister wouldn't have really let them fly me down that shaft. But it frightened the devil out of me, and I learned to sit quiet—or at least to not get caught.

Punishment was swift and certain: whacks on your open palm with a thick ruler as many times as the teacher saw fit. In fairness, the nuns did give us a choice. It was up to us to decide whether to hold out our left hand or our right to receive justice. But if we felt the sting on our hands, we did not feel the sting of race. Black or white did not matter. The nuns and priests disciplined us equally.

But I soon found that the world was a lot meaner outside the cocoon of my neighborhood if you were black.

As a young boy of ten or eleven, I decided I should start bringing money home to help my mom. When I saw a Boy Wanted poster for a job delivering telegrams for Western Union, I imagined myself a breadwinner, biking around town carrying telegrams with important news. I all but ran to apply, only to hear, "We don't hire colored boys here." That stung worse than my mother's slaps. My surprise was matched only by how protected and naive I had been. From then on, I was keener about slights and angrier about prejudice.

As I got older, I experienced more prejudice. One summer, I ventured out of Harlem and enrolled in a school in downtown Manhattan. I remember my excitement when we were told to bring swimsuits for an outing the next afternoon. I imagined the cool water. I saw myself splashing and laughing with the other kids, just having fun. My excitement built as we marched to the train station, but when the time came to put my fare into the turnstile, I was told to step aside. Before long, when I looked around, all my classmates had left—except for one other black kid. The pool, wherever it was, wasn't open to the likes of us. Racial prejudice was so ingrained in daily life that the teachers never showed a thought about leaving us behind. It's just the way it was. Looking back, I think they should have pulled us aside the day before to tell us the truth about swimming day (or better yet, they shouldn't have taken anyone swimming unless we could all go as a class). But I guess they just weren't sensitive to the daily humiliations black people faced every day. That was eighty years ago, and it still hurts.

Another day, walking home from that same school, white classmates followed behind me with the taunting chant, "Jesse Owens, Jesse Owens!" If I'd been a trackman being compared to Jesse Owens, the hero of the 1936 Olympics, it would have been an honor. But I wasn't a runner. Those kids might as well have called out, "Nigger, nigger." I settled the issue the only way I knew: squaring around and daring the white boys to take me on. When one was pushed forward by his buddies, I hit him with a swift punch to the jaw.

There were more of them than of me in that confrontation, but I had a bigger stake in the outcome than they did, and that punch made my commitment clear. It took the heart out of my antagonists and showed me the power of standing my ground. It also was among the first inklings of an important rule that I called on to keep order in jails: act fast and let them know you're in charge.

My lessons in authority and racism continued in the army, which pulled me out of college at St. John's University in Brooklyn and offered me the chance to see the world at war. The segregated army of the 1940s was a lesson in bigotry. I was initially trained for medical duty, but upon transfer to Fort Patrick Henry in Virginia, I joined other black troops as ditch diggers under the euphemism of "medical sanitation." Fort Patrick Henry was a port of embarkation where troops received final training before they were sent overseas for combat. At that time, the army believed black soldiers were suited only for menial duty: cleaning up after white soldiers, carting their equipment and gear, and generally toadying behind. German POWs seemed to get more respect than black GIs. The POWs marched around camp looking smart in their uniforms while I dug holes in slop and mud. At movies on base, I got hup-hupped by armed MPs to the back ten rows where blacks were supposed to sit. The camp commander shamelessly insisted he was bound by local Southern rules for segregating the races and giving black soldiers the worst of everything.

It didn't stay that way. Sometimes, somebody decides not to take it anymore. One movie night, things changed. A newly arrived black unit sat near the front, ready for the show. Confronted by white MPs with guns and bayonets drawn, these black soldiers left the show, returned to their barracks, and armed themselves, letting it be known that they were ready to fight for their rights on base. That show of force persuaded the local commander to ease discrimination on the base. From then on, we could move fairly freely on base, though the strict segregation enforced by the local citizens applied off the post.

I believe that incidents like these (they happened on other bases, too) were one reason that the army's two black combat divisions (the 92nd and 93rd) were stationed in a remote part of Arizona before they were sent overseas. I think fourteen thousand armed black men who were willing to fight were just too scary for the army's top brass.

But for me, Arizona looked a lot better than Fort Patrick Henry, so I volunteered with a couple of my buddies to join the 92nd—the first black unit that the army deployed for frontline combat. We were racial pioneers who fought German troops in Italy for the better part of two years, and I am damn proud that I could help show that black soldiers could perform in combat just as well as whites.

My time in the army, and especially in Italy, was a big part of the real-world education that I would turn to as a correctional officer. I found that you could talk truth to senior authority—at least if you picked your spots well.

In Italy, I was assigned to the medical corps with the authority to send soldiers to the rear when I believed they needed a break from combat. And, sometimes, I jumped in to help the local people. When a round of mortar practice began killing sheep and other village animals, I told the sergeant in charge I was going to run ahead and tell the civilians to get their animals inside. The sergeant said that I could run ahead if I liked, but he wasn't going to stop the shelling while I did so. I snarled back, "If you do that, you better not be here when I get back." And, though it was against the rules, whenever I felt it necessary to send a soldier from the front lines back to headquarters, I would take his place. I had to ensure that we weren't one man short when we went out on patrol. I would swap out my Red Cross medical helmet and replace it with a regular army helmet. I then would carry both my medical bag and a weapon. The lieutenant was actually pleased to see that I could cover two roles at once.

As much as I disliked the army and the racism I experienced, I also learned to separate individuals from institutions and to judge people on their own merits. Many white officers treated me fairly and with respect, including one who kept insisting that after the war he would get us together to go march through Georgia and set things right. We never did, of course, but I knew that man's heart was right.

When the war ended, I was glad to get home, put down my gun, stop killing, and start building my life. In 1949, I married Muriel Edmead and began raising a family—two beautiful daughters. Sixty-five years later, we're still together.

Roy and Muriel Caldwood's Wedding in 1949

One thing I didn't do was go back to school. I had a family to support, so I hooked on with the post office. For seven unhappy years, I toted a big, heavy Saratoga mailbag and delivered the mail. That was hard, hard work.

I spent all day long on my feet with that damn bag over my shoulder. It was eight hours of walking door to door, up and down the stairs of New York City apartment buildings with a bag that weighed almost as much as I did.

So when I saw an advertisement for correctional officers, it was a chance to get rid of the mailbag. I didn't honestly know what a correctional officer did, but I figured, *It's got to be better than this.* I checked it out and liked what I found. I thought it might even be a chance to help out young people who were in trouble.

Though I was small at five-foot-seven and only about 135 pounds (too short to be a police officer), the Department of Corrections held the door wide open. I walked through that door and wouldn't walk out for another twenty-one years. That's the story I'm about to tell.

CHAPTER 3

Hart Island and City Jail

1955. I'd been out of the army for almost ten years. I had a wife and a daughter, but other than that, I hadn't made much progress. As I headed for my first day of training as a correctional officer, I hoped that this would be the start of a satisfying career. The first days weren't promising.

I'd been through army basic training, and while it wasn't fun, it was certainly serious. The stakes were high, and the intensity of our training matched the mission. I couldn't say the same for New York City's program for turning civilians into COs. With a few dozen other young men, I was turned over to Captain Kolko for two weeks and a course that we dubbed "Kolko's College of Knowledge." In truth, there was no college and little knowledge. Other than learning to handle a shotgun, training pretty much consisted of reading manuals on jail rules and procedures.

Instead of the three *R*s of elementary school, we were supposed to learn about care, custody, and control. But we weren't taught how to translate those core elements into reality. Nor did we discuss the concept of "correction," or the idea that improving inmates' long-term prospects and deterring them from future crime was part of the job. The message was just to give orders, like little dictators, without worrying what the prisoners felt or thought.

So, I was fortunate that my early assignments were in relatively benign institutions with a small number of inmates who were in jail for nonviolent crimes, often involving alcohol. That gave me a chance to observe and learn with less pressure than there might have been. Also, like the rest of society, I think prisoners of sixty years ago were a bit less likely to directly challenge authority than prisoners are today. Certainly, some inmates were more difficult than others, and bad things happened in prison back then, too. But in my early years, the danger and level of violence was lower than when I retired. That gave me time to get my feet on the ground.

My first assignment was at the Long Island City Detainee Institution. There were only about fifteen inmates per floor and a hundred altogether. It was quiet and well run, and the prisoners were segregated by race just like in much of the outside world. I was only there about a month, but I did manage—on my very first day—to drop a set of keys through an opening in the floor. They fell down to a group of prisoners three floors below. With a mad dash down the steps, I snatched the keys back, saving myself from deep embarrassment and a likely dressing-down from the warden. It's funny now, looking back, but it wasn't the smooth beginning I was hoping for. As I watched the keys tumble, I wondered if my first day as a CO might also turn out to be my last.

Long Island City was a detainee location for inmates awaiting adjudication. That's also where I first witnessed the delirium tremens (DTs, or alcohol withdrawal). In this case, it was a raging, hollering prisoner demanding to be let out because he was late for work.

City jail wasn't tough duty, all things considered, but I was put to the test early—mostly by the warden. In my first week, I was given the special assignment of running the kitchen. When I told the warden I didn't know much about running kitchens, he told me to figure it out. "You might be new, but you're not ignorant," he said. I wasn't sure about it at the time, but I learned to appreciate the value of figuring things out for myself. In another instance, a senior officer responsible for searching inmates who were returning to jail from the exercise yard ordered me to get a comb from a young inmate with a tough reputation. I never knew why that comb was so important, but I marched up to the young man and told him I wanted it. Without any resistance, he turned it over. I found out then that even in jail, if you act like you're in charge, most people will go along.

The exercise yard was misnamed, as it had no exercise equipment. It was just a long cement path where the inmates were ordered to continuously walk back and forth until it was time to go back inside. It reminded me of my days in Italy, where the residents in many communities would come out of their homes and *pasagare*—walk up and down. The difference was that their walking was voluntary.

In those days, wardens lived in their institutions. One time, the warden took his Doberman pincher to the yard gate to release him for exercise. But the warden fell into conversation with the gate officer, and didn't release the dog for his run. After waiting patiently for a while, the dog made his impatience clear by biting the officer on the leg.

There were other unexpected dangers. One of our trusted inmates was assigned to replace light bulbs in a tower high up over the yard. But a police officer patrolling outside the wall thought it was an escape attempt and drew his gun to keep the inmate inside. Our trustee was so frightened he fell off the ladder and into the yard.

My next stop was Hart Island, a slightly bigger facility on a small island in Long Island Sound. It was also known as the workhouse where sentenced inmates served less than six months, and it was only accessible by ferry from the Bronx. As in the city jail, most of the Hart Island inmates were charged with alcohol-related offenses. We put them in dormitories, deloused them, and kept them warm. During the winter, street people would line up outside hoping to be let in. To some of them, Hart Island was a shelter, a safe place to go when street life got too tough.

For me, it was a place to learn my new craft, to figure out how to deal with prisoners, and to maintain order so the institution could run smoothly. It had its peculiarities. A rabbi who was serving time there was assigned to a private dormitory room and given kosher food that had to be brought in daily by ferry. And, if you dropped a half-smoked cigarette on the ground, you'd find inmates grabbing for that butt even before you could stamp it out. But compared to the places I worked at later—the Tombs and Rikers Island—Hart Island was easy duty.

At Hart Island, we had an old Irish officer. He called everybody "Laddie"—inmates, COS, everybody. He'd make the coffee for the inmates. But he only knew how to make it black.

He had a rule that you could eat all the bread you wanted, but you couldn't take it out of the dining room. If he caught you leaving with bread, he'd stop you and say, "Laddie. I see you're hungry. We don't want that. Eat up, eat up. Stay here and eat it ALL up."

I guess keeping food out of the living areas was important to him. Food was something inmates might fight over if one had it and one didn't. It also might attract mice and rats. Those were bad things that he wanted to keep out of the living areas.

The warden treated me fairly although I was black. In fact, **the Tombs was the only institution in my experience where the assignment captain would never put a black officer in charge of a floor, no matter how much experience or seniority the officer had.** Even the greenest white officer would get authority over any black colleague when this captain was in charge.

But even at Hart Island, the treatment of inmates was less enlightened. Black inmates were always assigned to the hardest, dirtiest work: shoveling coal for the island's power house or digging graves at Potters Field, a section of Hart Island where the city buried indigents when no family member claimed them. If family showed up belatedly to claim the body, the black inmates were sent out to dig them up. Black prisoners dug and shoveled; white inmates worked as clerks.

Hart was also the place where my philosophy toward prisoners and how to work with them began to take shape. To succeed as a correctional officer, it's a good idea to have an approach you believe in.

To me, the key was respect—I would demand it from the prisoners, and I would return it back to those who gave it to me. But in my early days on the job, I misunderstood what respect really was, and I went about it the wrong way.

I fell back on what I learned from my mom—a quick backhand when sassed, or even when not. But what worked between me and my mom, in a relationship based on love between parent and child, wasn't the right answer for a correctional officer dealing with hundreds of strangers who often didn't like him very much.

I'm a relatively small man. I was much shorter than the average American man even back then. I wasn't going to intimidate anybody into obedience with my size. That wasn't a particular problem in my daily life outside the jailhouse walls, but I believed it might handicap me as a CO. When a big guy gives orders, most folks are inclined to say, "Yes, sir," as a matter of self-protection—there's no reason to risk angering a larger man.

But I never worried that when they looked at me, prisoners might say to themselves, "Who's this little fella telling me what to do?" I believed that in order to have a recalcitrant inmate comply with orders, a quick slap was the way to go. My job was to protect all inmates, the weak form the strong. I never tolerated inmates taking advantage of others. When that occurred, I would bring the bully to my office and let him that behavior would not be tolerated in my cell block area. When I noticed a grin or smirk on his face, I would quickly give him a hard backhand slap. When he walked back to his section, his bravado walk was gone. I had made my point.

On a daily basis, new inmates were arriving on my floor. There was always one of them who I needed to let know that "we don't have any gorillas on my floor". "It might look like a zoo, but it isn't". Almost every day I had to repeat the same process to break in the new tough guys. By the end of the week, I was completely worn down and had no patience left. By Friday, when an inmate would approach me with an issue or concern, I had to turn them away and say "I've had enough".

What I came up with instead was an approach of mutual respect. After I got my footing, I operated on a simple premise: no matter the differences that had brought us together, the inmates and I were equally human. That may seem obvious, but in the environment of a correctional institution, it is anything but. The relationship between officer and prisoner—a captive deprived of the most basic freedoms and a captor who directs another man's life—is unnatural. It changes the way we interact. *Just give them orders* was the thinking of the day. And, for many officers, that was the way it worked. I disagreed then and disagree today.

Over the years, I learned that behavior that worked in the outside world often worked well in prison as well. Most prisoners feel the same emotions as the rest of us. Inmates worry about their family, the same way I do; they feel love, fear, and anger; they often feel bad about the bad things they have done; they enjoy music and art; and some like to read while some don't. Showing that you care works on the inside just like on the outside. During my time as a CO, I learned to listen to their complaints and consider their suggestions for making daily life a little bit better. I couldn't fix their problems outside of prison, but sometimes I could help them with things on the inside. And why not? **It didn't cost me anything to have patience, lend an ear, or even make adjustments that made the day a bit better.**

In return, they could offer cooperation that helped the institution run more smoothly and calmly. They might even give you enough respect that when you found yourself in danger, as I did when taken hostage, an inmate would pay you back by saving your life.

So when it made sense to me, and despite head shaking from some of my colleagues, I let prisoners out of their cells and gave them a little taste of normalcy even when it was against the rules. I didn't do it to break the rules, but because it seemed like the right move at the time. Late in my career when I had enough influence, I organized an arts program, arranged for entertainment by popular musicians, set up a prisoner basketball league, and even arranged a few weddings. **Drawing on my own humanity to help prisoners when I could turned out, at least for me, to be far more effective than ruling with fear or just barking orders, as some colleagues thought I should.**

I didn't become the inmates' friend; I didn't try to fix their lives, lecture them on how to be a better person, or counsel them on how to succeed on the outside. I just tried to help them get by day to day. My job was to keep the institution running in an orderly fashion, to keep the prisoners safe from one another, and then to deliver the prisoners back to society at the end of their sentences.

I also wasn't there to enact some additional justice or punishment beyond what the court decided. These men had lost their freedom as their designated punishment. It wasn't my job to add more.

Why they were there, what crime they'd been convicted of, or what charges they would be tried on really didn't matter to how I went about my job. I didn't want the temptation of easing up on somebody I thought might have been wrongly or excessively punished. Nor did I want to exact some additional justice or make life needlessly hard for somebody whose behavior on the outside offended my sense of right and wrong.

When each man came in, we started fresh to develop our own jail-based relationship. I would demand respect and return it back. I would expect them to follow the rules and do what I asked—basic chores like cleaning their cells and making their beds. **I let them know I would help them when I could, but it had to be a two-way street. I'd tell them, "I can't do anything more for you than you allow me to do."**

If they would not go along, I would have to find ways to cajole them into cooperation—or at least to prevent them from disrupting the institution, creating trouble with other prisoners, or making my work harder than it needed to be.

I began to test my approach at Hart Island—not in a planned way, but just day by day as it made sense. I skirted the rules if my gut told me there was a better way. Sometimes I got good results; other times things didn't work out quite so well.

One of our main jobs at Hart Island was helping inmates dry out from the drunkenness that often brought them there. I spent much of my time witnessing prisoners get through withdrawal (the DTs), which wasn't easy for them or pleasant for me.

Sometimes the doctors would provide sedatives or other medications to smooth out the process, but with or without medical help, the withdrawal usually happened in the prisoners' cells. They probably should have been in an infirmary or hospital where a doctor or nurse could keep an eye on them. But for the most part, the prisoners had to get through it on their own—except for the times when COs would step in to try to make it at least a little bit safer.

One time, I made the mistake of going in a cell with a prisoner during withdrawal. You weren't supposed to enter a cell by yourself in that situation. But I opened the door, thinking I should retrieve the man's dinner tray before he started tossing it around. When I did, that man decided that instead of me coming in, he'd like to come out. The DTs can make prisoners very agitated and excited. They may hallucinate, seeing things that aren't there. And in this excited state, they seem to gain extra strength—or at least a fierce determination that makes them hard to overpower. When this guy came barreling out, I put my hands to his chest but soon realized I couldn't stop him. So, I decided to "join" him. "Come on out," I said. "Let's go get a drink."

I began walking toward an imaginary bar, leading him along. "Let's go to the corner," I said. In his agitated state, it seemed a reasonable idea to him even though the "corner" would just put us at the end of the cellblock. Then I stopped and told him we'd gone the wrong way. "Wait a minute, wait a minute. It's this way," I explained as I turned to walk him back toward his cell. Stride for stride, we walked together like best buddies going to share a drink. He was into it, imagining that first cool swallow of a favored brew. I am sure he forgot we were in a jail. Then, with his guard down, we came to his open cell door. I summoned all my strength to shove him back inside and quickly slammed the cell gate to keep him there.

That could have meant my job. I can only imagine the trouble he might have caused if I couldn't get him back in the cell. I sure didn't want to explain to the warden how I'd let that man get out.

Sometimes, nothing I did was enough. Often, inmates in withdrawal would have imaginary fights, real ripsnorters, as they boxed at shadows and cursed at some invisible foe. In rage, one inmate began tossing his metal bed frame around the cell at some unseen enemy. With another officer, I went inside the cell to get that bed out. We wanted to stop the noise, which was riling up the other inmates, and also to keep the man from hurting himself. For a while, the fighting died down, the noise faded, and I went back to my rounds to check on other inmates. Then it started again: the man was having it out with a new enemy. Without a bed to throw, he charged at his imaginary foe headfirst into the unpadded concrete wall and knocked himself out, stone-cold dead.

CHAPTER 4

A Day in Jail

The fundamental challenge for a correctional officer is that prison inmates are not happy, and that their unhappiness makes them harder to deal with. This unhappiness is compounded by a daily routine of extreme regimentation, orders, and boredom. There's no doubt in my mind that some prisoners "act out" just to inject some interest in their day.

"The Snake Pit" Inmate Drawing

A typical day might go like this:

7:00 a.m.—The prisoners would be up for breakfast and marched to the dining hall in small groups under the gaze of a correctional officer, while other officers would check them at several points along the way. They would be told when to sit, when to rise, when to pick up their silverware and tray, and when to return them. In my time at Rikers Island, every moment of the morning meal was carefully choreographed to help the officers keep inmates under control. Later, as Rikers became more crowded, we began to provide "room service" by bringing meals to the cellblock instead of taking inmates to the meals. That reduced the security risk, but it also frustrated the inmates by taking some variety out of the day.

8:00 a.m.—The prisoners would be locked back in their cells for the first "count" of the day. They would stand in front of their cells so an officer could count them and check the tally against the previous count, which would have been taken by an earlier shift of officers around midnight. We had to make sure that every prisoner was accounted for and that there were no escapes (or deaths) in the night. Sneaking out of jail isn't easy, but from time to time prisoners would manage it. As a CO you need to know with each shift change whether anybody has gone missing.

8:30 a.m.–9:00 a.m.—When I ran a cellblock, the next activity after morning count was cleaning. I wanted cells cleaned and mopped. I also believed in making beds just like I learned in the army. And the bed making had to pass my inspection or I'd expect the prisoner to do it again. Such chores might seem beside the point for a prison inmate, but I believe keeping living quarters in good order provides a bit of normalcy in a grim situation and nurtures a small bit of positive pride—even in jail—that makes the men a bit more cooperative. It was also a way to try to keep the prison a bit healthier and hygienic. Penal institutions tend to be damp and dark. Ventilation is not ideal, and back then there was no such thing as climate control. That made penal institutions good breeding grounds for colds, cough, and flu—not to mention lice and other vermin. Keeping the cells and cellblocks clean was one way to help fight off such afflictions. Frankly, it was also a way to remind the inmates that I was in charge.

10:00 a.m.—With the count finished and beds made, the inmates would be on their own out of their cells, free to move around in the cellblock and sometimes in the exercise yard. Some would be taken, under guard, to court appearances. Rikers Island, where I worked for about fifteen years, houses a small public school that inmates can attend. Others would go to the library to read a book or to the law library where they could work on their cases. Some would just mill around on the first floor of the cellblock, "the flat," chatting with other inmates or playing cards and trying to get though the day.

If the institution had a gym, inmates might go there, though for large portions of my career, the gym was way too small to fit all the men who wanted to use it. At Rikers Island, we had to parcel gym time in assigned sessions. Two times a week was the most gym time available to any individual inmate when I was at Rikers, and sometimes it was less. During my career, with more and more men doing time, New York City's jails were chronically overcrowded, and the exercise yard would get so jammed that we had to build small mini-yards between buildings so the prisoners could get some fresh air.

Noon—This was time for lunch, but first the inmates would go back to their cells for another count. Then we marched them in groups to the dining hall, generally a cellblock at a time or a portion of the block if it was one of the larger ones. In my later years on the island, we brought the food to the block.

1:00 p.m.–3:00 p.m.—With lunch over, it was free time. The prisoners would be locked out of their cells and could move in the block. They couldn't stay in the cells; they had to be out. That was one more example of control. It never made sense to me. If a man wanted some alone time in his cell, I didn't understand why the system said no.

3:00 p.m.–6:00 p.m.—The prisoners would be locked in again so the next shift of COs (4:00 p.m.–midnight) could start their workday with yet another count to check against the earlier totals.

6:00 p.m.–7:00 p.m.—Dinnertime. The inmates would have been counted by the new shift and locked in for several hours, and now it was time to let them out for another meal. They'd be counted again after dinner and then let out again.

7:00 p.m.–9:00 p.m.—The final lockout and "free" time of the day.

9:00 p.m.–7:00 a.m.—Bedtime. The inmates would be locked in until the next day's breakfast. The midnight shift of officers would do one more count when they arrived—this time peering through the bars of each cell and counting the sleeping bodies. That count required the officers to look closely to figure out whether the figure under the covers was a breathing human being. You did not want to find out later that what you thought was an inmate was just a pile of clothes or some other bulky material bunched up under sheets to camouflage the rare escape.

Then, the next day, we did it all over again—day after day after day.

The free time, of course, is welcomed by the inmates, but it's the hardest part of the job for the officers. That's the time when COs are most vulnerable—confined in a cellblock and badly outnumbered by a group of unhappy and often angry men. Jail inmates are typically a younger group, mostly under forty (with a large group in their twenties), and there are relatively high numbers of aggressive men. They have lots of energy and few positive ways to work off steam, which increases the odds of fights among inmates and attacks on officers. An unusually high number, perhaps as many as half, have mental health or behavioral problems that also make fighting more likely. In short, it's a tense environment, a snake pit in which prisoners are ready to battle with each other or with the officers. Every form of bad behavior—including rape, assault, and drug abuse—that happens on the street also happens in a correctional institute. Seemingly benign activities may often hide something bad. For a time at Rikers, inmates would bring sheets and blankets from their cells and throw them atop the long tables where they sat for card games. The men said the coverings kept the cards from sliding off the table as they dealt. The blanket hung down to the floor, and they hid sexual assaults and rapes that took place beneath the tables. Once we figured that out, we imposed a new rule against table coverings. A rule against table covers probably sounds like micromanaging bureaucracy—unless you've spent any time in jail.

Any time an officer intervenes, there's the chance he will trigger a larger confrontation or even a riot. And when I was working in New York City jails, there was usually no way for an officer to easily summon help. For the most part, officers were on their own, relying on their wits and self-policing among the inmates to keep the place more or less under control. In the old Rikers pen, the officers in the block couldn't even give each other much support. The two corridors did not connect except at the very front of the block. If you thought help was needed on the other side, you had to run to the front of your side to get to the other officers' section—and by the time you got there, it could be too late. Not to overstate the problem—most officers made it through the day and went home without any physical wounds—but it's an emotional drain to worry about that day after day.

There simply weren't enough officers to stop or even see all the misbehavior that went on. Near the end of my time at Rikers Island, a cellblock might hold three hundred or more prisoners (about twice what they were built for) and would be patrolled by three officers per shift. One of those officers was assigned to the front of the block and served basically as a receptionist who logged prisoners in and out as they went to and from court appearances, meetings with attorneys or social workers, class, gym, the library, or other activities in their free time. That left two officers to keep an eye on the prisoners in the block—an area divided into two sides, each a football field in length, and several tiers. No matter how alert, the officers couldn't possibly see all that was going on. Bad things could happen that they simply wouldn't be aware of no matter how hard they tried to be everywhere and see everything.

One thing that didn't happen very much when I served in the correctional system was the sort of education, training, or other social programs that would have given real meaning to the word "corrections." The daily schedule allowed some time for inmates who chose to go to school or to spend time in the library. At Rikers, we usually had an inmate magazine or newspaper that a few prisoners would work on, often with the help of outside volunteers. But attendance at these programs varied. Systematic efforts at corrections such as job training, assistance with job search, or assistance in transitioning back to freedom weren't featured on the daily schedule.

As an officer, just trying to keep the place running was a full-time challenge. And that may have been the biggest personal disappointment of my career. One of the reasons I was attracted to prison work to begin with was the possibility that I might be able to help young men who had started down the wrong path. I didn't get to do as much of that as I hoped.

Correction should be the system's second most important goal after protecting society. And if we want to provide the public with long-term protection, we could make it the top priority. There's a good chance that an uncorrected criminal out on the street after serving his term will go back to breaking the law. In fact, more than half of released prisoners are rearrested within one year of getting out of jail, and more than three-quarters are back in trouble within five years.[5] That may be the best proof that putting people behind bars doesn't really work very well.

We've been talking about "correction" for a long time in our country. For example, the charter for the Massachusetts Bay Colony way back in 1629 spoke of "lawful correction" for those who broke the law, and the founding document of the American Correctional Association (ACA), the national organization of correctional officers, says the system's "great object should be his [the prisoner's] moral regeneration."[6] That was back in 1870. In 1960, when I was still early in my career, New York City Correction Commissioner Anna Kross, one of the best to hold that job, discussed her efforts to shift from "a mere custodial agency to that of a rehabilitative, re-educational, and correctional one."[7] Today's ACA principles say: "Corrections is responsible for providing programs and constructive activities that promote positive change for responsible citizenship."[8]

It all sounds good. But in practice, whatever correction takes place is in spite of an inmate's time in jail, not because of it. Putting a criminal on the straight and narrow is hard work, and it takes a lot of resources, especially money that isn't readily available.

The inmates I dealt with were more likely to spend their time inside learning how to be better criminals, teaching each other new ways to do

---

5 US Bureau of Justice Statistics, "Three in Four Prisoners in 30 States Arrested Within Five Years of Release."
6 "History of United States Prison Systems," Wikipedia, http://en.wikipedia.org/wiki/History_of_United_States_prison_systems, November 2014.
7 Department of Correction, City of New York, Seventh Annual Report, 1960.
8 American Correctional Association principles, November 2014 http://www.aca.org/aca_prod_imis/ACA_Member/AboutUs/Dec.aspx?WebsiteKey=139f6b09-e150-4c56-9c66-284b92f21e51&hkey=a975cbd5-9788-4705-9b39-fcb6ddc048e0&Principles=5#Principles

illegal things and how not to get caught. **For many prisoners, jail was a chance to exchange information about better ways to rob, steal, peddle drugs, and hustle the street.**

And that was true even for men who weren't committed to crime when they came in. Imagine what happens to a young man who is suddenly put in jail and kept there while awaiting trial. If he had a job when he was first detained, he would likely lose it by the time he came out—even if he was ultimately found innocent or the charges were dropped. There aren't too many employers that hold a job open for somebody in jail, especially if the job doesn't require special skills and the wait for the worker to come back may last several months.

Inmates are largely cut off from their families. They can't support partners or children while in jail, and they also may lose the family's emotional support. By putting men in jail, we destroy the so-called "community ties" that might give an inmate the incentive to stay on the right side of the law. For a young man who may have been struggling to get by to begin with, putting him together with criminals at the same time he's cut off from family, job, and friends may help push him to the wrong side of the law. **Instead of a correction system, what we've got is a complication system.**

CHAPTER 5

Overcrowding, Riots, and Other Hazards

There's an unspoken problem with throwing people in jail. We wind up with more prisoners than cells to put them in, which makes it a lot harder to run correctional institutions the right way. In the later part of my career, the jails in New York City were badly overcrowded, making life a lot more dangerous for correctional officers and inmates alike, and also reducing the odds of corrections activity that would help prisoners turn their lives around.

At both Rikers Island and the Tombs, we routinely had to double up inmates in cells meant for one. Toward the end of my career, when I was an assistant deputy warden at Rikers, we were housing about 1,500 detainees at a time in the detention facility, but our effective cell capacity was just over 1,300. More than three hundred inmates were typically doubled up—two men in a five-by-eight cell designed for one. The ceiling was in close, too, and an average-sized man could put his hands flat against it. In a word, it was suffocating. From time to time when I was at the Tombs, we were forced to put a third man on the floor. Sometimes, one of those inmates was an alcoholic or drug addict going through withdrawal, and he might be throwing up on the floor, making an already miserable situation even more miserable. As you might imagine, nobody was very happy about that.

Cramming inmates together in that way creates tension that leads to riots. I am certain that's why there were several significant uprisings during the final years of my career, as overcrowding got worse. The fewer people you lock up, the easier it is to keep the jails calm.

A special report to New York City's Board of Correction in 1975 said overcrowding was the biggest reason for growing tensions at Rikers House of Detention for Men (HDM). The report blamed overcrowding for "creating an environment that is in a perpetual state of emergency." It added: "There is common agreement among correctional experts that overcrowding is the single most significant contributor to inmate unrest and an increase in institutional tensions. Nevertheless, HDM is overcrowded."[9]

---

9   "Report on the New York City House of Detention for Men," June 1975 (prepared for the City of New York, Board of Correction).

New York Post

FOUNDED BY ALEXANDER HAMILTON IN 1801

DOROTHY SCHIFF..Editor-in-Chief and Publisher
JAMES A. WECHSLER......Editorial Page Editor
PAUL SANN..........Executive Editor
ROBERT SPITZLER....Managing Editor

Published daily except Sunday. Owned by the New York Post Corporation, 210 South St., New York, N.Y. 10002. Dorothy Schiff, President. Byron S. Greenberg, Treasurer. Joan Cillene, Secretary.

Explosion on Rikers Island

There may have been a time when conscientious judges believed that a judicious prison sentence could help assure the rehabilitation of a prisoner. That impression is not widespread nowadays. Similarly, it will require appreciably more than an order of the court to reform a prison.

Those realities, the daily burden of correction specialists, have been thrust into public consciousness once again by the latest New York City prison rampage—the 17-hour revolt on Rikers Island that began last Sunday night, after a slow, steady, sinister buildup in recent months. The courts in question are not city or state; they are federal.

No sensitive, well-informed witness to the situation—correction officials, guards, prisoners and private citizens were among such observers—would dispute the indictment of prison conditions here by such jurists as Federal Judges Judd and Lasker.

Their findings that prisoner overcrowding is an offense to the Constitution conform fully not only with this country's legal traditions but with the judgment of prison authorities, who view crammed cellblocks as the single most explosive element they face.

Yet 300 of the Rikers cells were doubled up as the riot broke out.

Why? The basic explanation is that the city simply could not afford the expense of carrying out the judicial decrees.

Thus, when Judge Lasker found The Tombs unfit for human occupancy, the city was forced to make a choice between renovating that grim relic or closing it and moving prisoners to Rikers. In other words, there was no choice: there was no way of paying for the restoration and the prisoners were shipped to the island.

The federal courts' judgments have been eminently sound. They cannot be meaningfully enforced unless the federal government is prepared to contribute substantially to that goal. No anticrime rhetoric in Washington offers a substitute for tangible programs.

In the aftermath of the Rikers riot, denunciation of the amnesty terms under which the hostages were released was inevitable. But such critics were silent during the fateful hours when human lives were at stake. Would New York have preferred another Attica?

The crucial issue is not "capitulation" to rebellion. It is the avoidance of those desperate circumstances in which officials confront the grim choice they faced during the Rikers revolt.

N.Y. Post Newspaper Article November 1975

The immediate problem at Rikers was created when Federal Judge Morris Lasker forced the city to close the Tombs because of bad conditions there. But shutting the Tombs just shifted the problem to Rikers. Moving prisoners from one bad jail just turned a functional institution at Rikers into a troubled one. The jails just kept getting busier and busier. And it got much worse after I retired in 1976.

At the start of my career in 1955, there were about 180,000 inmates in all of America's state and federal prisons. Even by 1976, the national inmate population was about 260,000. That's when the big explosion happened as policymakers embraced a "law-and-order" agenda to drive down crime and clean up an epidemic of powerful street drugs such as crack cocaine. By 2011, state and federal prisons held some 1.6 million men and women. County and city jails held another 730,000.[10] Among the biggest reasons for the increase were drug crimes. Between 1980 and 2011, the number of prisoners serving time in federal, state, and city facilities for drug crimes climbed from just over 40,000 to about 500,000.[11] Though the prison population has declined for the past few years, the United States remains the world's number-one jailer with about 2.3 million locked behind bars in federal, state, and local correctional institutions. I

---

10 "How New York City Reduced Mass Incarceration: A Model for Change?" Brennan Center for Justice, the JFA Institute, and the VERA Institute of Justice, January 2013.
11 The Sentencing Project, "Trends in US Corrections," November 2014, http://sentencingproject.org/doc/publications/inc_Trends_in_Corrections_Fact_sheet.pdf

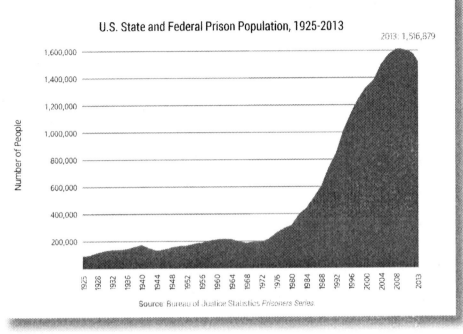

Trends in U.S. Corrections

New York City followed a similar path. The average number of inmates locked up at any one time rose from about 5,200 in 1950 to 9,000 in 1960.[12] By 1991, New York City's jail population had soared to 22,000, but then the city started to reverse national trends, and the inmate population moved down to 14,500 in 2001 and to fewer than 12,000 today.[13]

Overcrowding changes the dynamics of an institution. The rule book, such as it is, goes by the wayside because it was written for a set of circumstances that no longer exist. If possible, you try to take the real circumstances and turn them to your advantage. At times, I found that

---

12 Op. cit., Department of Corrections, p. 32.
13 Op. Cit. NYC—Mass Incarceration study, p. 32.

I could use the housing situation as a tool to let inmates know that I was in charge.

There are all sorts of ways that a CO can establish that inmates will be better off if they get along with him. In an overcrowded facility, cellmate assignments are a big deal. Cells are all pretty much the same; some might have a slightly better view of what's going on, and some inmates might prefer to be at the end of the cellblock because it's quieter. Others might want to be in the middle—closer to the action, as it were. But generally, cell A vs. cell B doesn't matter much. Whom you bunk with, however, can be a very big deal.

When I was at the Tombs, one of the white inmates complained bitterly about sharing his small space with a black man. Being black myself, I could have taken it personally. To tell you the truth, that white man's attitude did annoy me a bit. But being judged harshly by an inmate didn't keep me up late at night. I mean, why should a little prejudice be a surprise coming from a man who may have a long list of character issues? Not to mention the fact that complaining about black people wouldn't seem a good strategy when appealing to a black officer. But I was willing to play along—or let him think I was.

"Of course, of course. I see the problem," I assured the man, whose name was Smith. "I can put you in with a white guy if it will keep the peace."

Of course, white or black, there are some folks you just don't want to room with. And that's exactly what I had in mind. I thought, *Mr. Smith, meet Mr. B.O.*—as in body odor. He was a bum who'd been picked up on skid row and tossed in jail. And he was a bum in jail, too.

I found the foulest-smelling white inmate I could. I walked Smith down the cellblock and stopped in front of his new cell. He balked. I asked what the problem was, because I'd found him a white cellmate. He still didn't move when I told him, "Get in, or I'll throw you in."

The stench was so great that no amount of scrubbing could ever purify that cell. That inmate, who'd had the cell to himself, never bathed that I knew of. I'm not sure how he could stand his own odor. A couple of days with his new cellmate, and Smith would have bunked with just about anybody else of any color. He came to me desperate for relief. He was so desperate that he volunteered for work on the house gang, the inmates who did the dirtiest, toughest work in the jail. They were mostly black, but compared to his foul-smelling roomie, Smith decided they would be great companions—and they had individual cells. It was a true jailhouse conversion, and I like to think that I was responsible for a great stride forward in racial tolerance. I never had any trouble with Smith after that.

Back then, separating people by race was still the rule in much of the United States. This was the 1960s. The civil rights movement was stirring up society on the outside, and a lot of white people were resisting demands for integration. Some black people preferred separation, too, at least when it was their own choice. So, it wasn't all that surprising that one black prisoner, a black Muslim, told me he didn't want to bunk with "Whitey." I put him in with Poet Green, a tall, proud black man. That might seem like a perfect match, except that Poet Green liked to quote from the Bible—loudly and all night long. He didn't care whether you listened or not. He didn't care what your religious heritage was. He had a captive audience, literally. And he was going to preach—on and on and on and on. A few days of this—up all night with little sleep and biblical verse pounding in his head—and Poet Green's new cellmate wanted out. "Get me out of here," he pleaded. I said, "I've got a cell, but the other guy is white." "I don't care," the inmate assured me. Almost whimpering, he repeated, "I don't care. Just get me out of here."

But I would have happily given up that little edge in exchange for easing the population crisis. It's hard and dangerous work to have too many inmates to care for, to feed, to watch over, and to control. Health care, which may already be deficient, is strained. Sick inmates or troubled ones don't get the attention they need; grievances—large and small—are pushed to the side by the authorities but irritate prisoners even more. It's harder to make a phone call, take a shower, or get access to the gym, library, or exercise yard. Small incidents blow up into big ones. A bump is a reason to have a fight. In early 1972, the stress helped produce a riot at Rikers Island. I came out of that riot as something of a hero, but I would have preferred if it never happened at all.

It was the first of February 1972 when the riot alarm sounded. Three officers had been attacked in cellblock seven, which was housing about three hundred teenagers waiting for trial. I was elsewhere in the jail giving a tour to some administrators, but I excused myself quickly to see what was going on. I'd been in that block often and knew some of the leaders, and I figured my help would be appreciated. Of course, it's pretty much all hands on deck when there's trouble in the block.

By the time I arrived, we'd already fired tear gas into the block. Putting that burning, stinging gas into somebody's lungs and eyes can take the fight out of a man fast. Instead of pushing forward aggressively, gassed prisoners are likely to pull back and reconsider their options.

Deputy Warden Harris was in charge, and I asked, "Dep, what's happening?" He explained that we had injured officers. They'd been attacked by the inmates in the block but had managed to make their way out. The inmates were armed. Though tamed a bit by the gas, they didn't appear ready to give themselves up.

Deputy Harris hadn't alerted the warden yet, hoping he could settle things down quickly on his own. But faced with a standoff, we agreed it was time to tell Warden Jim Thomas that cellblock seven had rebelled.

Thomas had worked his way through the system to become the first African American warden in New York City. He was a tough guy who would use force if necessary but preferred to find more peaceful solutions whenever possible. In his mind, one of his top responsibilities was to keep officers and inmates alike from getting hurt. He was a terrific man with whom I had a great rapport. In the end, getting Thomas to the jail that day proved to be one of the smartest things we did.

By this time, the prisoners had retreated to the rear of the cellblock to try to get away from the gas, and they were huddled behind barricades of torn-up furniture. We were outside the gate and badly outnumbered, trying to figure out how we could regain control of the block.

Harris thought of me as a softie, a peacenik, because I gave the prisoners some respect. I surprised him when I volunteered to take a look. In all the confusion, nobody had the key to the cellblock gate. It was six or seven feet high, but I climbed up and waved to the inmates at the back. One of them shouted, "Hey, that's Captain Caldwood up there."

I took that as a friendly sign, so on impulse I leaped down into the block to have a closer look. I didn't really have a plan. I'd always followed my gut instincts. It just felt like the right move. There wasn't time for long analysis; I had to act fast.

On careful review, my actions might not seem the smartest because inmates are a mixed bag. Even though I treated them with respect and had a good rapport with most of them, there were always a few who might kill me if they got the chance. But too much analysis can freeze us from doing anything at all, and that wasn't an option. We had a situation that needed to be resolved, and I thought I might be able to do it.

The inmates were armed. That wasn't a surprise. **Weapons find their way into jail. No matter what you do or how much you search, there**

will always be weapons. The inmates had added to what they could smuggle in by adapting the things you find around a jail. They took pipes apart. They took beds apart. Mops and broom handles can be converted into weapons, too. They'd broken up furniture and toilets and shaped knives out of bedsprings. Every one of these standard jail items can injure a man when an angry person has it in his hand.

Handmade Inmate Weapon

Young and full of testosterone and resentment, the inmates could hurt a lot of officers if it came to a fight. I had no doubt my side would ultimately win because we could draw on vast resources as long as any fight lasted. But it would be painful. A lot of officers and inmates would be injured, and some might die. I ignored catcalls from some inmates who shouted, "Keep him back here," meaning me, and set out to see if I could bring this thing to an end.

I found the leader, Cuba, who weeks later would make me a hostage. I had a tear-gas mask, but Cuba didn't have one, so I took mine off to show we were in this together. It was the sort of small gesture that I think creates a bit of trust. I told him the situation as I saw it: "They've already fired a lot of gas back here. There will be more. But so far, nobody's been killed. Listen to me, and I can get us out of here without that—before anybody is in bad trouble."

I wasn't dramatic. I didn't make any threats. But Cuba was willing to avoid a fight, too.

His terms were straightforward: address our grievances, or at least hear us out, and promise that there will be no retributions if we put down our weapons and come out. "If they promise not to beat us, we'll give up," he offered.

To me, a quick yes was the only reasonable response, but when I took word back to Deputy Harris, I was in for a shock. "I can't promise them that," he said.

I was stunned. To me, there was no doubt that yes was the only answer that made sense. To these inmates, it was a gang fight, and they were ready. The officers had little batons—no guns or other weapons—and the inmates were up to their eyeballs with knives, iron pipes, table legs, and broom handles. This was a fight we ought to avoid. We could have peace by saying yes.

I was mad—seething, actually. I didn't know what to do. I turned my back and stormed away. I couldn't go back and tell Cuba, "You are going to get beaten." With that kind of message, the inmates would hold me there for sure, and I might even end up dead.

Deputy Harris shouted at my back, ordering me to turn around. I ignored his command, deciding to let him put me on report if he would. I'd risked my life by going into the block on my own to begin with. I wasn't about to double down by going back with bad news.

My insubordination ended when I heard the booming voice of Warden Thomas: "Captain Caldwood, what's the situation?" He had just arrived at the block. Thomas and I often thought alike, and it was true this time, too. "Of course," he assured me. "Go back and tell the inmates we can make that promise—no retribution, no beatings, no violence." Thomas's terms were simple: drop the weapons and walk out.

I took the warden's answer back to Cuba, told the inmates to drop weapons and line up by twos, and marched them out of the block to the auditorium where they would be searched. There were forty officers with batons facing 120 inmates with assorted handmade weapons. As we marched, more weapons fell to the floor—they'd been held in reserve in case the warden broke his word or any officer ignored his orders and started swinging. We walked by a gang of officers summoned for a possible assault. I'm sure some of them wanted to get in some swings to avenge their injured colleagues, or just because they saw an opportunity. But they didn't defy the warden or break the rules of the truce. When the blows didn't come, the prisoners began to trust a bit, and I could hear some remaining weapons clanking on the floor. For that moment, I had secured peace.

The warden put me up for a commendation on account of "intelligence, bravery, and a complete disdain of the possibility that he might have been taken hostage and seriously injured or even killed." He also noted that I had previously contributed to the "easing of tensions" between inmates and officers. I wasn't motivated by recognition. I just wanted to go home safe after a day without violence. But I appreciated the gesture. It's always nice to be thanked.

Making the Right Moves: Rikers Island & NYC Corrections

GMA — (8-65 20M)   Department of Correction — Intradepartmental Memorandum
                                                                   #257

Date   : May 16, 1972

From   : Warden, N.Y.C. Adolescent Remand Shelter

To   : Commissioner of Correction

Subject: RECOMMENDATION FOR DEPARTMENTAL RECOGNITION OF CAPTAIN ROY CALDWOOD, SHIELD NO. 235

1. On February 1, 1972, approximately 120 inmates of Cell Block #7 rioted within the aforementioned cell block at approximately 1:30 p.m. During the riot Captain Caldwood distinguished himself in a manner deserving of departmental recognition, as follows:

2. When the riot alarm was sounded, Captain Caldwood responded to Cell Block #7. By the time he arrived, due to the prior use of tear gas, all of the rioters had gathered behind barricades that they had erected in the rear half of the "A" section of Cell Block #7. It should be noted that the rioters had necessitated the use of the tear gas due to their unprovoked attack on three Correction Officers which resulted in injury to each. A great majority of the inmates behind the barricades were armed with home-made weapons made from broom and mop handles, stilettos made from bed springs, broken pieces of toilets, chairs, etc. The fact they were armed was clearly discernable from the front of the cell block. The situation was at a standstill awaiting the arrival of the Warden. Without receiving orders to do so, Captain Caldwood, unarmed and alone, proceeded to the area where the inmates were barricaded. He reports that when he arrived at the barricade the inmates were quite truculent, threatening and yelling revolutionary slogans. After conferring with the inmate leaders for approximately ten or fifteen minutes, Captain Caldwood was successful in getting a promise that if the Warden would guarantee that no physical reprisals were taken against them, they would lay their arms down. In the meantime the Warden had arrived at the front of the block. When he observed that the inmates were conferring with Captain Caldwood, he halted all preparations to use force pending the outcome of Caldwood's efforts. Acting on Captain Caldwood's assurance, the inmates laid their arms down and slowly marched to the front of the block lead by Captain Caldwood. Captain Caldwood then informed the Warden, who was present, of the negotiated agreement and the Warden approved. The inmates were taken out of the cell block into the auditorium corridor without further physical incident. It should be noted that Captain Caldwood on several previous occasions, has substantially contributed to the easing of tensions between large groups of belligerent inmates and the custodial force.

3. Captain Caldwood's performance, as described above, entailed intelligence, bravery and a complete disdain of the possibility that he might have been taken hostage and seriously injured or even killed. There is no question in the Warden and Deputy Warden's mind (both of whom were present) that the brave action of Captain Caldwood prevented serious injury to additional personnel and inmates.

4. In view of the above, it is recommended that the Department recognize the commendable actions of Captain Caldwood, as described above, by awarding him the Departmental Honorable Mention Award, in compliance with Departmental Rule #5.69.

JAMES A. THOMAS
Warden
N.Y.C.A.R.S.

Warden Commendation Letter May 1972

Ending that uprising was possible only because I had treated prisoners with respect and earned some credibility and trust in return. But I didn't feel any elation. As I marched the prisoners to the auditorium, I listened to their chatter. I didn't like what I heard. They still had the same grievances. They were disgruntled and angry. **Absent some miraculous change in prison conditions, I was certain another riot was only a matter of time.** The jail was still overcrowded. The prisoners were still unhappy about the way they were treated and the conditions in the jail. I had helped end this uprising before anybody was seriously hurt, but instead of elation, I felt foreboding. I was pretty certain that all I'd won was a temporary peace. Sooner or later, I knew the prisoners would rise up again—only longer, harder, and with more determination.

CHAPTER 6

Hostage No More

I was right. I had helped end the uprising in early February, but nothing had been resolved. The prisoners' grievances hadn't been addressed. Four weeks after Warden Thomas said yes to Cuba's deal for short-term peace, I was Cuba's hostage. Two of my officers had their necks in a noose. I had to find a way out.

So, I shouted for Cuba. He was my lifeline, my best hope. If I lost him, if he lost control of the inmates or of his own good sense, some of these guys would kill us all. A disturbance in jail can take on its own momentum. Things can happen that weren't planned, and plans can change. The longer we were in, the more the inmates could get tired, anxious, or fearful. And tired, anxious people often do stupid things.

I was nearly frantic to stop it somehow, to turn off the tear gas and get the prisoners to quit before the officers came in to end the revolt with violence.

I was counting on Cuba's air of command. The other prisoners would listen, providing I could convince him to back off—or get the warden to call pause. "Cuba, I've got to *see* the warden. Not on the phone. I can't get through. You've got to let me go see him face to face. I can stop this before anybody dies. If you kill me or any of my officers, my guys are gonna come in, and all of you are going to die. Do you want to die? I gotta stop this first."

Something clicked. Perhaps Cuba started to realize he held a losing hand. Whatever the reason, Cuba hooked my arm, and off we went. Down the stairs to the flat, which was jammed now with inmates like the subway at rush hour. Up toward the front, by the barricaded gate, the inmates huddled together. They were expecting a fight even though the gas had made them a little less eager and even though they couldn't win—not in the long run. Once the signal was given, officers would come in waves, and reinforcements would follow until the inmates were beat. That's how it works in jail. That's what institutions do.

Cuba and I squeezed our way toward the gate. We clawed between inmates, around them, and even beneath their arms. We angled our elbows out to push and prod and create space where there wasn't any. "Get out of the way; get the hell out of the way," I shouted. Cuba shouted, "Move, move, move, you SOB," and shoved people aside. I got to the barricade, but now I was blocked. The big scaffold had to be moved for me to get out. It was too big, too heavy, and I couldn't make it budge.

Somehow, I had to get to the front. I'm small, and maybe I could find a way out. Maybe I could lose myself in the bodies and crawl out before anyone noticed.

Up on the barricade, alone, atop the mattresses and the scaffold, a big inmate was swinging a heavy iron pipe. Officers were at the gate, trying to push into the cellblock. Every hand that came through the bars, every finger was a target, and this guy was mashing at them—*bam, bam*—and getting quite a few. His back to me, I reached up to try to keep him from hurting the officers. At my touch, he turned. He raised the pipe. *I'm dead for sure*, I thought. I closed my eyes for the blow. Nothing. I opened my eyes and looked again. He was gone. I didn't know why or where he'd gone, but he'd vanished into the chaos. He hadn't hit me, and that gave me my chance.

There was a space between the scaffold and the gate, just enough room for a small man, and I squeezed my body in. On the other side, officers grabbed me and pulled—whether I was an inmate or an officer didn't matter. They could get one person out of the block, either to save him or to catch him.

I was out.

It'd been two hours, two long hours, since I'd been taken.

I was full of adrenaline after forcing my way through to freedom. Four brother officers were still on the wrong side of the bars, two with nooses around their necks. A rescue force was ready, but it would be a hard fight and bloody. Better to end this without a nasty charge and the wounds that would come with it.

I was still thinking I could stop this if I could just talk to the warden.

Fast as I could, I raced toward the control room to tell the warden to stop, to call off the assault. The prisoners would quit, I was sure of it. At first, they'd wanted a fight, but the water and gas had cooled their fire a bit. If they were so set on fighting, I figured I could not have gotten out. We could stop the gas, pull the officers back from the gate, and let the prisoners calm down and give up. I believed it could happen.

Out of breath, I found the warden. "You've got to stop this! They'll quit if we let them," I insisted. I told myself it was true.

Then the two of us were racing back to the gate, me in my T-shirt, the warden in his suit. "Stop, stop," we yelled, our hands up as a signal to call it off, that the war was over. But it was too late. We couldn't be heard. The commotion was too loud, and no one paid us any mind—if they even noticed us at all. There was a fight going on.

The officers were on a mission. They were determined to free the hostages before it was too late. They aimed to subdue the prisoners and regain control, and hurt them, too. They were forcing their way into the block, and the prisoners were trying to come out—grunting, screaming, clubs swinging. Pipes, wood, and steel smacked bodies. Inmates threw chunks of metal and toilet tanks and seats—whatever they could rip free.

I caught a riot baton in my ribs. Taking me for an inmate, an officer had smashed my side. With my uniform gone, it was an easy mistake in the melee. The pain took over my body as if every rib bone was shattered. I was a wounded animal, wanting to kill the one who hit me. He was big, mean-looking, and intimidating, with a helmet and black-tinted visor hiding his face. But I was too raged with hurt to be smart, and I wanted to hurt him back.

I leaped at my prey, but two other officers, six-footers, intercepted me. One had my left arm, and one had my right. I was pinned, helpless, and the guy who hit me readied another blow. Fists clutched around the club, he wound up. His brain told him I was an inmate who deserved another shot.

Up, up the club went above his head. He squeezed it tighter still. For the fourth time in the day, I thought, *I am dead*. Then, another officer recognized me. His yell couldn't be heard through the mess, so urgently he pressed his mouth to my attacker's ear: "No, no, it's Captain Caldwood. Our guy," his lips mouthed. In a burst of comprehension, my attacker eased off and brought the club down to his side.

The other officers released their holds; first they freed my right arm, and then they let go of my left. But I was still enraged, and the pain in my ribs pushed me to hit back. I charged—but at no one. My attacker had moved off to find a real inmate to hit.

And then it was done. The assault team went in and got the other hostages out. They recaptured the cellblock and locked most of the inmates back in their cells. They took out the leaders they could identify. Cuba was dragged out, stiff as a board with fright. He was scared to death now and afraid he would be beaten. He was just a kid, really, not more than twenty years old. Now, bravado gone, he was just a frightened young man. They all were.

Just dumb stupid kids. They'd made a mistake. They thought a tantrum would make things better. When I calmed down, I felt sorry for them. They were locked in jail and serving time—months or more—even before a trial or a verdict. Unable to make bail, they had no one on the outside to help and no one on the inside who could make changes. Whether guilty or innocent, they were already doing their time. "Sentence first, verdict later," the Queen of Hearts said in *Alice in Wonderland*. At Rikers, it happened all the time. No wonder these young men were angry.

They had acted from desperation. In the end, they just earned themselves more charges, more time behind bars, one more line on their rap sheets. It's the way it works: start a riot in jail, assault officers, and take hostages, and the system is going to make you pay.

CHAPTER 7
Force and Violence

Riots and hostage taking don't happen often, but these occasional outbursts remind us that correctional institutions can be violent places—and that violence leads to more violence. I think most people agree that when prison inmates take hostages, the institution has the right to use force to restore order. That doesn't mean storming a cellblock at the first sign of trouble. It's much better to end an uprising peacefully, as I helped do when adolescent inmates took over cellblock seven in the first part of February 1972. But that isn't always possible.

There are a few other times when force is justified. If an officer is assaulted by inmates, it may require force to stop the fighting before an officer is hurt badly. Inmates will hurt each other, too, and it may require force to keep them apart.

In fact, the mere threat of force helps keep jails peaceful. If it wasn't for that threat, jails would be extremely disorderly because inmates would routinely ignore or defy COs. If an inmate doesn't do what he's supposed to—move along in line or get in his cell for lock-in or a count, for example—you may have to use force to get him to comply. To be clear, "force" is not the same as hitting or beating. It may simply mean grabbing an arm or shoulder and directing an inmate to get moving. If an inmate won't get in his cell when he's supposed to, a CO might have to push or drag him in. There are different degrees of force, and a good CO will use the most minimal force necessary to get the job done.

Nobody likes to get hit (or pushed), and inmates will generally go along with orders rather than risk being hit. So, the possibility of force is a deterrent that helps keep jails operating pretty smoothly.

This deterrence also makes jails safer for officers by making it much less likely that an inmate will assault a CO. Inmates know that hitting an officer is a dangerous thing to do. Hit an officer, and you can count on being hit back with greater force and often by many officers. When I was at Rikers, all bets were off when an inmate hit an officer. Warden Thomas was adamant that we weren't supposed to hit an inmate once a fight ended. If you stopped the brawl and the inmate was under control, he was supposed to be safe. But some officers didn't follow the rules and would continue to hit an inmate after they should have stopped. I didn't see that happen very often, but inmates knew it was possible, and fear kept most of them from crossing the line. They just didn't want to take the chance.

Still, some inmates couldn't or wouldn't control themselves. I was never hurt badly, but prisoners hit me on several occasions without warning or provocation.

One time at the Tombs, we were escorting Catholic inmates to confession. The priest had set up a small confessional in the front of a room, and we would bring the prisoners into the room a few at a time and sit them on benches while they waited their turn. When one man was finished, the next guy in line would walk to the confessional, close the curtain, tell the priest what was on his mind, and ask forgiveness.

The priest said we should leave the front row of benches vacant to make sure that the confessions remained private. He didn't want to take the chance that an inmate who was sitting too close might overhear what was said in the confessional. We respected that request, and so did the inmates. Confession was an important ritual for many of them, something they practiced regularly on the outside and were pleased they could continue even in jail. They also wanted privacy, so sitting in the second row (or even farther back) was not a problem.

At least that's what we thought, until one guy plopped himself in the front row. Thinking he hadn't understood the rules or just forgot where he was supposed to sit, I signaled him to move back a row. But he stuck in his seat. I signaled again and got the same nonresult. *What was wrong with the man? Was he just being defiant? Or did he just not understand?* I walked over to find out, and as soon as I got there, he jumped from his seat—but he wanted to fight, not move.

He threw up his fists and started to dance on his toes as if he were Muhammad Ali. Then he dropped his hands, stepped forward, grabbed me in a bear hug, and pinned my arms to my sides. The other inmates shouted, "Let him go, let him go." They were there for confession, not trouble. He pulled his arms clear but shoved me a bit as he let go.

"I want you outside," I told him. He followed me through a swinging door to the hallway, where I thought we could talk it over while letting the confessions go on. I let him go through the door first, but when I walked through, I saw he was back in his fighting pose. He charged, fists swinging but wildly out of control. I ducked away and hit him hard. The commotion could be heard in the next room, and in moments another officer and the priest burst through to see what was going on. The inmate complained that I'd hit him.

"Damn right, I hit you," I said. "You were coming at me with your fists—what'd you expect me to do?" He was subdued by now, rubbing his jaw and no longer interested in fighting. So I asked him why he hadn't moved from the front row. His answer was to the point: "I didn't want to."

That was that. I guess he was bored, or tired of taking orders.

Another time, at Rikers, we were taking prisoners into a secure area. That meant passing through a very cramped doorway into the cellblock. It was nothing out of the ordinary, though, and things were going along just fine. The inmates moved quickly and efficiently in single file to where they were supposed to go. About a dozen had passed by me without incident when one of them deliberately stomped on my foot—hard. He didn't just graze me, and it wasn't an accident. He'd landed square on my foot and with more force than a typical step. It smarted like hell, so I grabbed him. "Why did you do that?" I asked.

He answered by trying to throw me to the floor. The next thing I knew, we were both on the floor inside the block, right by the gate, and tussling good. I was able to get him in a headlock, but I didn't want to let go because he might try to hit me if I did. By now, other officers had run up to help. But they were on the wrong side of the locked gate and couldn't get in. I had a key, but it was hard to get to while fighting. The gate officer who should have been there to let them in had ducked into the restroom a few moments before. Sensing something wrong, he dashed out of the john—but before buttoning up his pants. So there he was, holding up his pants with one hand and trying to pull the gate keys from a pocket with the other. It just wasn't working. It would have been funny except I was on the ground wrestling with a prisoner. I wanted some help. Somehow, I managed to get a key out of my pocket while keeping my grip tight around the inmate's head. I flipped it through the gate to the officers outside, and finally they let themselves in.

They broke us apart and got that inmate back to his cell. They were a bit rough with him, but not excessively so. He was luckier than other inmates who hit officers. Sometimes they would get beaten up badly. We are supposed to protect inmates, so getting in extra licks when you have a man subdued is wrong. But when you've just been hit or seen a fellow officer who's been hurt, some people lack the self-control to do the right thing. I saw a few such incidents and made some enemies among fellow officers by not taking part and, at times, trying to cool things off. As I moved up in rank, I could and did order officers to stop when they were going too far.

But excessive force and deliberate and unnecessary violence by COs against inmates was a relatively rare occurrence when I worked in jails. It may have happened once a month. That was too often, of course, and the wardens should have stopped it. But it wasn't the routine practice that some may imagine and that some reports say happens at Rikers today. I can't say this strongly enough: **the type of violence and brutality that reports say is systematic at Rikers today was not an issue when I was there**. The grievances that most concerned prisoners during my time on Rikers were the basics of daily living. Court orders to fix the Tombs and Rikers focused on matters like recreation, overcrowding, medical care, and visitation rights. Violence by COs was not high on the grievance list.

Every profession has a few bad apples, but I believe the vast majority of COs aren't interested in beating inmates. **More than anything else, what COs want is a peaceful day. Unless you are seriously out of whack in your own head, beating people isn't fun.** Harassing inmates or riling them up until they argue and fight with you isn't fun either. It's stupid. It can get you hurt or killed. I can't understand COs who want to do that.

It's also unnecessary. You can do your job, get prisoners to cooperate, and keep the institution running smoothly without violence. Treat the inmates with respect, address their legitimate grievances, and show that you have their interests at heart, and most of them will do what you ask. It took me a while to learn that, but I am certain it is true. I know it worked for me.

There's another issue of violence that tends to get less attention but that makes a jail or prison a worse place to be. That's when inmates attack inmates. Correctional officers are supposed to protect inmates and keep that from happening. But it isn't always easy to do, and the violence can't always be predicted. During my service, inmates were more worried about being hurt by other inmates than about attacks by officers.

One time at Rikers, we were processing new prisoners for their first day in jail. You don't really expect serious trouble when you do that. It's a pretty routine process—give them a number and a cell, tell them what's expected, and help the new men get settled in. They haven't been together long enough for any feuds to exist among the new arrivals. But trouble can come when you don't expect it. This day, we were putting a new guy into his block when one of the inmates who was already in jail made a crazed dash, lunged at the new guy, and stuck a knife in his gut. After we got it all sorted out, I asked the man who did the stabbing what it was all about.

"I know that guy. Took him in when he didn't have any place to live. Gave him food and some clothes. And then he robbed me blind. I swore that the next time I saw him, I was going to get even."

I had no way to predict that or prepare for it. You just can't know when two guys have a beef.

CHAPTER 8

Inmate Grievances: They Were Real

Considering their unpleasant existences, it shouldn't have been surprising that the adolescents at Rikers had revolted. The real surprise was how long it had taken them to do so. They had a long list of legitimate grievances. Medical care was bad. The food was barely tolerable. There weren't enough showers. Access to families and lawyers was limited. Inmates couldn't even make phone calls. Instead, any message to a family member or an attorney was filtered through an officer who would pick up a phone and relay news or ask questions based on notes from the inmate. That was on top of the overcrowding.

At Rikers Island, the vast majority of the glass windows were broken, so birds would routinely fly in and out of the building. This bit of neglect actually provided all of us with a bit of relief from the drudgery because the inmates would turn those birds into pets. The birds made their nests in the upper section of the cellblocks. Prisoners would take baby birds from the nests and train them to sit on their shoulders. Unlike the inmates, the birds could fly in and out at will, but most of the time they would return to their cellblock homes. The men called their pets "jail birds."

Still, the broken windows illustrated the broader disrepair, and the bad conditions weren't a secret. Just three days after the February 1 uprising in 1972, a special report from the state of New York said housing, health care, and education conditions at Rikers were unacceptable. The report threatened to withdraw our state certification. Nobody who had been inside a jail—COs, wardens, senior administrators in the correctional system—could disagree. We all knew things were bad.

And at a detention center, inmates are further frustrated because they had been deprived of their freedom even though they hadn't yet been convicted of anything. Here's what the city's own Board of Corrections said about conditions at Rikers in the early 1970s:

"First, the inmates are detainees, men still presumed to be innocent and awaiting trial. They are being held for months at a time, uncertain what will eventually happen to them, virtually cut off from family, friends, jobs, and community."[14]

As a prisoner, your mental outlook is always down. It was tough on the COs, too, but at the end of the day, we got to leave. Getting back to my wife and children always revived me enough to go back again the next day. Inmates, of course, don't go home. They faced the deficiencies 24-7.

Medical care, for example, was awful. We didn't have enough doctors, and the ones we had often weren't very good.

Some of the doctors had physical limitations that made it hard for them to do their jobs well. One was legally blind. He was a sweet man with the right skills, but he had to push his face almost up to a piece of paper to sign his name. It was hard to believe he could do a thorough exam.

---

14   Op. cit., Department of Corrections, p. 32.

Other doctors were arrogant or visibly disliked the prisoners they were supposed to take care of. I remember one doctor who insisted on giving a penicillin shot to a CO even though the officer said he was allergic. "I am the doctor," the physician persisted, with an emphasis on the word "I" and extreme annoyance at being questioned. He gave the shot anyhow, and, predictably, the officer wound up in the hospital.

Another physician treated the prisoners like "untouchables" and tried to conduct exams while standing twenty feet away to keep himself safe. I don't know how the hell he could provide good treatment with an attitude like that.

Most of the prisoners were stuck in jail because they were too poor to post bail. If you have the money for bail and good lawyers, you get to keep your freedom while awaiting trial. There's nothing wrong with that. In fact, it's generally the way it should be. But that wasn't true for the poorer inmates that I dealt with every day. For me, that would have been grievance enough to rebel if I had been on the other side of the situation.

The inmate uprisings of 1972 also reflected the mood of the times, including a general feeling among many Americans that authority existed to be challenged. Protests—against the war in Vietnam, racial and gender discrimination, and "the system" in general—were in the news and on the streets every day. The inmate population included a growing number of Black Panthers and black Muslims, who were steeped in the idea of shouting out. More than forty people had died in riots at Attica prison just a few months before the turmoil at Rikers, and most of New York City's other jails had experienced a wave of revolts in October 1970. The Tombs, the Brooklyn House of Detention, the Queens House of Detention, and the Long Island City Jail, where I'd started my career, all blew up in violence. The Rikers inmates, rising up about eighteen months later, were actually late to the party.

Some argue that getting locked up before trial isn't such a big injustice because most of the inmates turn out to be guilty. Knowing that, many defense attorneys would delay trial as part of their legal strategy. For a guilty man, the hope is that delay will open the door for a plea deal with a shorter sentence than he would have gotten if he lost at trial. Delay also fogs witnesses' memories, and some who might testify die or move away.

It's true that most detainees are ultimately found guilty, but for those who aren't (one old study says that a quarter or more are acquitted),[15] it's a huge injustice to spend any time in jail at all. Innocent until proven guilty is one of our country's most important principles. But at Rikers and every other detention center, that premise is violated every day. It still burns me up more than thirty years after I retired. It's also one more reason to treat inmates with respect. What if they didn't do it? They'd already lost their freedom. We shouldn't take their dignity, too. It wasn't my job to anticipate and mete out more punishment in advance.

My job was to keep things under control, but it was hard to blame the prisoners for acting out. So I worked inside to try to make it better, to listen to what they said, and to fix what I could. After the first 1972 uprising, I was given a more formal role in making Rikers work better when I was part of a committee that met with prisoner representatives to talk about their concerns. Records of those meetings show how long the list of grievances was, how basic most of them were, and how little we could do at the institutional level to deal with them.

To the inmates, grooming and personal care mattered a lot, just as on the outside. The men complained there weren't enough showers (there weren't), and that the ones we had frequently weren't working. Toilet paper was often in short supply. The prisoners said it was too hard to get a haircut

---

15 "Pre-Trial Detention in the New York City Jails," Columbia Journal of Law and Social Problems, 350, 1971, Content downloaded/printed from HeinOnline (http://heinonline.org), Thu, Jun 19, 13:59:49 2014.

(we had 1,200 inmates and eight barbers, so, sometimes, there would be a wait). The mess hall was a regular target for complaints—too many hot drinks in the summer when the men wanted something cold, and shortages of basic items like cups and bowls. Dietary concerns reflected the growing Muslim population, which worried there might be pork in food such as hot dogs and salami that was labeled as beef but might not be. Allegations about mislabeling might sound like paranoia except we were in a place where a package of meat said "all beef" on one side and "pork" on the other"?—We never did find out which label was right—or whether both of them were wrong.

4-20-74
10-1-74

— Open Discussion —

W/s the Inmate Advisory Committee Request to see Commissioner or a representative from his office to discuss the following items:

1) The installation of a telephone for "self-use" in each side of a block.

2) Instituting a fund for bail, using a percentage of the commissary profits and the "Recreational Equipment Fund".

3) A more varied and Kosher Food selection in commissary

4) Improved medical facilities, medicine and care, plus access to immediate medical attention

5) Improved equipment for the maintenance of the "housing-areas", immediate repair of the windows, plumbing and electrical malfunctions. A designated day, and the proper equipment, for the cleaning and pressing of clothes

— Open Discussion — "con't"

Inmate Advisory Board Request

There were complaints, too, about the lack of jobs, excessive lock-ins and lockouts, and the handling of the prisoners' mail. The prisoners suggested an increase in rehab services to give them a better chance on the outside. The administration acknowledged that the rehab and training opportunities weren't adequate. We agreed to ask headquarters for more, but we had little confidence that such services would be increased.

The inmates asked for fans and better ventilation, especially in the visiting areas so their families would be more comfortable. They suggested that prisoners should be put to work to keep showers, dining areas, and recreation areas clean. That would give them something productive to do, too. They wanted more time in the outside recreation area, but we didn't have enough officers to provide security for that. And they asked for the right to make at least one phone call a month—a real phone call during which they could talk directly for themselves without filtering their conversation through an officer.

Some might say, "So what?" or argue that the prisoners had earned their discomfort. But the goal of prison should be to give the inmates a better chance when they get out. In other words, "correction." Ideally, we would use the time that men spend in jail to educate them, give them skills, and teach them how to survive—legally—on the outside. That kind of rehab begins with allowing them to feel human. Brutalization, even if unintended, is far more likely to harden them with resentment and increase the odds they will break laws again.

~ OPEN DISCUSSION ~

cont

5) A more hygienic condition for serving food in the blocks, and a better prepared, varied and choicer menu

6) A modernized and more extensive transportation system, and a less crowded busing proceedure.

7) The modernization of the visiting area, extended visiting hours and the instituting of contact visiting privileges

8) Better sanitary conditions and modernized plumbing and lighting in the institutional court-pens.

9) A area formulated for co-defendants visits and the granting of co-defendant visiting privileges.

10) Implementation of a non-mandatory, rather than mandatory busing policy, to other institutions for pre-trial detainment.

11) That a neutral onlooker and reporter be allowed to come to advisory meetings.

2

Inmate Advisory Board Request

CHAPTER 9

Jobs Can Help Keep the Peace

One of the best ways to keep a jail or prison from blowing apart is to offer jobs, or at least some form of regular productive activity. It's really just common sense. When people have something productive to do, it eliminates boredom and reduces tension. It also uses up energy that inmates might use for rebellious activity. Just think about the good kind of tiredness you feel after a satisfying workday or some strenuous activity that you enjoy. In her book *Orange Is the New Black*, Piper Kerman noted the monotony of her time without a job and compared joblessness to purgatory.

The ability to work is a big reason that a penitentiary, which houses convicted men serving their sentences, is typically a better place than a detention center for inmates and COs alike. I got to see the difference firsthand at Rikers Island, which was a "pen," or prison, when I got there in 1962 but changed to a detention center a few years later. There was more work for COs and more trouble after it stopped being a pen.

Because they were there for the long term, inmates in a prison could be assigned regular jobs—in a kitchen, on an outdoors work gang, in a garden, or on a maintenance crew. When I was first assigned to Rikers Island, **I was stunned to see civilian gardeners march off at the head**

of a crew of convicted inmates who were shouldering picks, axes, and shovels to tend to plants and raise vegetables, prune shrubbery, and engage in other agricultural activities. Those garden tools could easily become weapons, but the prisoners liked getting out in the fresh air to do something constructive. The work was good for their morale, kept them fit, burned off energy, and helped the day go faster. They didn't want to risk their jobs with bad behavior, so they tended to toe the line and cooperate. Just as in outside life, when people have something to lose—even a small privilege—they tend to take fewer risks.

The Department of Corrections summed it up like this in a report in June 1975:

"The majority of the penitentiary inmates were assigned to outdoor work gangs for most of each day. The location of a large segment of the population in one area facilitated supervision. Furthermore, the opportunity to leave the housing area and engage in outdoor activity served to reduce inmates' frustrations and anxieties."[16]

When most inmates are working, it has the happy side effect of making things better for the inmates and COs who are back in the cellblocks as well.

"In 1967, while the facility was still a sentenced institution, there were five officers assigned to a cellblock. Since many if not most of the inmates were on work gangs, the officers were often required to supervise as few as a hundred inmates within the cellblock during the day. This situation enabled the officers to provide more services for a much smaller number of inmates than is now the case," the Department of Corrections said in its 1975 report about operations at Rikers.[17]

---

16 Op. cit., Department of Corrections, p. 32.
17 Ibid.

At detention centers, by contrast, jobs are the exception. The population is too transient and unstable to establish work teams that would get anything done. About the only inmates with regular jobs in a detention center are those who have been convicted and sentenced but haven't yet been transferred to a pen to serve out their time. These so-called "time men" are often assigned basic tasks in the kitchen or on cleaning crews to help keep the institution running. While this might be considered menial work on the outside, most of the inmates liked having jobs—if only to relieve the boredom. Having nothing to do makes the misery of jail even more unpleasant. Without work, the time creeps by slowly, slowly, slowly. The prisoners' boredom is also a problem for the officers because the inmates are desperate for some action. "Action" often means behavior that breaks rules, tests the COs' authority and patience, and leads to fights among the prisoners for the officers to break up.

Prisons and detention centers differ in other ways than jobs. Security requirements are much greater in a detention facility because there is a much wider range of activities. The population at a detention center is changing constantly as new arrests are made, and those who can't make bail are sent to jail to wait for trial. That means moving large numbers of men into and out of a detention center every day. At a place as big as Rikers, we could have a hundred or more new inmates every day. At a pen, the men are serving longer sentences, and the population is stable. Only a handful are likely to be admitted at any one time. On some days, you might not have any new admissions.

There's also a lot more coming and going within the institution at a detention center. Because detainees are still awaiting trial, there are many more attorney visits than in a pen, where inmates have already been tried and convicted. You are constantly moving inmates in and out of the building for court appearances. Once it became a detention center, detainees at Rikers were allowed more family visits—twice a week, instead of once every two weeks in a pen. All of that movement requires officers for security. But toward the end of my career, the detention facilities at Rikers had fewer COs then when it was a pen, and the security requirements were less demanding.

One morning, after Rikers became a detention center, we had to move about a dozen inmates downtown for court appearances. We put them in the back of a paddy wagon, and two officers sat up front in the cab of the vehicle, where they were separated from the prisoners. One of the inmates specialized in picking locks, and he could work his way out of handcuffs as well. When the officers arrived at the courthouse and opened the door, they were surprised to find that all of their prisoners had been uncuffed during the ride. Without restraints, every one of them made a break for it, running through the courthouse to see if they could get to the street and escape. With the help of courthouse security and the New York City police, they were corralled before they got very far. That sort of thing didn't happen very often, but it illustrates the extra demands when you're in charge of detainees rather than sentenced inmates.

Even keeping clean or getting fed was a bigger hassle after Rikers changed from a prison to a detention center. When Rikers was a pen, for example, we marched all the prisoners to the same large bathhouse for showers and the same dining hall for food without reference to their crimes or the lengths of their sentences. We thought it best to separate inmates charged with homicides away from the rest of the inmate population. After Rikers was converted to a detention center, the older adolescents (ages 19-20) were separated from the younger inmates. For example, those accused of homicide were grouped together.

Most fundamentally, detention centers are inherently unstable because constant turnover in populations make routines harder to establish. Just as you begin to understand how to deal with certain prisoners and keep them under control, they move on. Inmates are either sent somewhere else to serve their sentences or released after acquittal or because charges are dropped. They are then replaced by new inmates that the COs have to figure out from square one.

Although those held at detention centers stay in custody way too long while waiting for trial, they simply aren't around long enough to establish the stable routines that can take hold in a pen. In a pen, where prisoners are held for several years, officers and prisoners become accustomed to one another. They learn to understand each other's personalities and habits and how to make the adjustments necessary to get along in a relatively peaceful way. In a sense, it's like living in a family—you may or may not like each other, but since you spend so much time together, you figure out ways to make it work. And because you know each other better, it's also easier to spot changes in behavior or routine that might be a sign that a problem is in the air. To be sure, plenty of bad behavior takes place in pens, too. Prisoners are always looking for ways to "get over", and COs must always be on the alert. But housing a stable population with relatively minimal turnover offers significant advantages.

CHAPTER 10

The Trouble with Bail

Even more fundamental than offering jobs, the fastest way to improve conditions in jails and prisons is to reduce the number of people we lock up. In that sense, penal institutions are like just about every other organization—the less stress you put on a system, the better it works. Smaller classes in a school usually mean better results. If you go to a restaurant, the service is faster and better if the waiter has fewer tables. In a prison, an officer can do a much better job of spotting and stopping trouble if he's responsible for thirty prisoners instead of three hundred. It's just common sense.

But throughout my career in jails and prisons, the number of prisoners kept going up, and the number of officers held steady or went down. That made it easier for inmates to assault or rape one another without an officer stopping them. Imagine one CO trying to keep an eye on three hundred inmates spread over a jail corridor as long as a football field. Too often, the damage is done before an officer can intervene.

It doesn't have to be this way. We just have to stop putting people in jail who don't belong there. I don't mean we should ignore crimes or stop arresting the folks who commit them. But we ought to find productive alternatives to locking people up before trial or stashing people in prison cells when they need treatment for mental illness, drugs, or alcohol. Supervised release and alternative sentencing that allows people to remain in the community, live with their families, and/or keep jobs would often make more sense than putting people in cells.

That would solve a lot of the problems prisoners complain about. Not enough showers? Too many people in a cell built for one? Rationed access to exercise yards or gyms because too many people want to use them? Those problems are solved when you cut the number of people in jail.

There would be less violence in jails and prisons, too. **Eliminate overcrowding and get the jail population down to capacity (or below), and there will be less stress and less tension—and that means people won't fight so much.** That's common sense. The Vera Institute of Justice, which advocates for prison reform, put it this way when studying New York City's efforts to reduce the number of people it puts in jail: "There is evidence that the reduced prison population created a safer prison system with less violence to inmates and staff."[18]

Reducing the number of prisoners is not as hard as some might imagine, especially when crime rates have fallen pretty steadily for the past twenty years.

A lot of the inmates I dealt with in jail were there because they were poor. I don't mean there was a deliberate policy to imprison poor people. But it's said that "bail equals jail" because an awful lot of people in detention centers in New York City and around the country are there because they don't have the money to post bail. Even when bail is relatively low, poorer defendants simply can't afford it.

Every day at the Tombs or at Rikers, I dealt with inmates who couldn't make bail—even when it wasn't very high. The New York County Lawyers' Association (NYCLA) has calculated that the average bail requirement is $2,000, way too high for the typical defendant, who is usually living below

---

18 Op. Cit. NYC—Mass Incarceration Study, p. 32.

the poverty line. Even when bail is set at $500, only about half of defendants can come up with the money. In New York City, the average stay—before trial—is almost two months.[19] Often the alleged crimes aren't very serious. According to the NYCLA, about 25,000 bail cases in New York City in 2011 were for misdemeanors or lesser violations such as trespassing, disturbing the peace, public drunkenness, and shoplifting. New York City police arrested 50,000 people for misdemeanor marijuana possession alone that same year. All told, Human Rights Watch says that about one quarter of people admitted to jail in New York City in 2008 were there because they couldn't afford bail.[20]

Keep those people out of jail, and the jails would run a whole lot better. We'd save a whole lot of money, too—about $42 million a year just on nonfelony defendants who were in New York City jails in 2008 because they couldn't make bail.[21] New York City spends $168,000 a year for each person it keeps in jail.[22] That makes it the most expensive jail system in the United States—by a lot. It's also nuts. That's enough money to pay for four years of college at a state university and about three years at the most expensive private schools.

Instead of just throwing people in jail, maybe we could use that money to give them an education or train them for a good job. Or we could spend it on treatment for mental health problems (a very high percentage of prisoners have mental issues), alcoholism, or drug addictions.

We could start by reforming the bail system—or even eliminating it altogether. The way the bail system works now isn't right.

---

19 NYCLA
20 "Bail Equals Jail: An Equation that Punishes New York's Poorest," *New York Daily News*, December 9, 2010.
21 Human Rights Watch
22 "City's Annual Cost Per Inmate is $168,000, Study Finds," *The New York Times*, August 23, 2013.

The system is often arbitrary. Sometimes judges require bail and sometimes they don't, even when the crime is the same and the defendants' circumstances seem similar. Some states are headed in the right direction, changing their bail system so that requiring a cash payment in exchange for pretrial release is the exception, not the rule. That's something that should happen everywhere.

By putting the defendant's money at stake, bail is supposed to ensure that defendants will show up for trial. But for the most part, that doesn't seem necessary. The vast majority of people who are let out before trial without cash bail show up for their court date even though no money's at stake. A number of bail reform experiments have shown that money isn't a big difference maker between who shows up for trial and who doesn't. A few years back, a program called the Bronx Freedom Fund raised money to bail out poor inmates who couldn't afford bail. Ninety-three percent showed up for trial—a higher rate than those who used their own money for bail.[23]

New York State's chief judge, Jonathan Lippman, says the current use of bail, at least in New York State, is "unfair" and "strips our justice system of credibility."[24] That man is right on.

There's one more thing about the bail system that drives me nuts: it's fundamentally wrong to keep people in jail until they've had a trial and been found guilty. In school, I learned that one of the best things about America is that you are innocent until proven guilty. That's why the US Constitution prohibits "excessive bail." The idea is that people should be able to go on with their lives and enjoy their freedom unless they've been convicted of a crime.

---

23 "Bail Is Busted: How Jail Really Works," *The Village Voice*, April 25, 2012.
24 "Top Judge Says Bail in New York Isn't Safe or Fair," *The New York Times*, February 5, 2013.

But every year in America, hundreds of thousands are locked up even though the law says they are presumed innocent. More than one in five US jail inmates are being held without a trial or a conviction.[25]

Bail requirements may make sense for violent crimes. None of us wants dangerous people walking up and down the street and putting the rest of us at risk. Even then, bail involves judging before a trial. But if the rules are clear and a court says it makes sense, protecting public safety is a defensible reason to require bail. That circumstance doesn't apply to most people in jail.

It's true that most of those being held will eventually be found guilty, and that the time served before trial will be applied against their sentences. But what of those who aren't guilty? We can't give them the time back, restore the income and jobs they've lost, or eliminate the pain for their families. They wind up being punished without cause. That's just flat-out wrong.

It's stupid, too. It costs money. It overloads the jails so that inmates' experiences are worse and more dangerous. It doesn't even make us safer—most of those who are locked up are in for nonviolent, low-level crimes that don't generally hurt other people.

Eric Holder, the US attorney general from 2009 to 2014, summed it up this way:

Almost all of these individuals could be released and supervised in their communities—and allowed to pursue or maintain employment, and participate in educational opportunities and their normal family lives—without risk of endangering their fellow citizens or fleeing from justice.[26]

---

25 Op. Cit. NYC—Mass Incarceration Study, p. 32.
26 Eric Holder, remarks to National Symposium on Pretrial Justice, June 1, 2011.

Fortunately, a number of states and local communities are finding better ways to enforce the law, arrest people who break it, and make sure the accused show up for trial without locking them in jail because they lack the money to pay bail.

There are a lot of ideas out there for keeping people out of jail before trial. States are substituting supervised release programs; monitoring defendants' activities; and sometimes enrolling them in drug rehab, alcoholism programs, or other social services while they are waiting for trial. Some states have made such pretrial release programs the first resort. Putting people in jail—"pretrial detention," to use the formal term—is reserved for special cases to be used only when there's strong evidence that the accused is a threat to public safety. With modern GPS technology, it's possible to let people live at home while also knowing where they are or restricting their movements to designated locations such as work or school. That still limits their freedom somewhat, but it beats being locked up in jail.

This type of pretrial release not only helps people keep their lives intact but it also saves money. Judge Lippman puts the cost of monitoring at $4,600 a year on average across the country, only about a quarter of the cost of putting somebody behind bars. **I'd much rather hire a probation officer of some sort to keep tabs on a defendant living at home than pay more money to lock somebody behind bars.**

I don't know the perfect answer. We probably need a combination of approaches, but I am certain we can do better. That would help empty our jails and prisons of people who don't need to be there—at least not yet—and eliminate a lot of the problems that are caused by overcrowding.

CHAPTER 11

Drugs

Everybody knows that drugs can create problems. Get addicted, and you may not be able to hold a job or support your family. Use too much or the wrong kind, and they can kill you. Run out of money to buy them, and you may turn to crime. They also put a big strain on the correctional system, loading up jails and prisons with a wide range of drug offenders. But there are a lot of differences among drug "criminals." Some are casual users, some are addicted, and some sell drugs for a living and commit violent crimes in the process. Yet we prescribe the same solution for all. We can be smarter than that.

In the 1970s, America decided to get tough on drugs. We passed new mandatory sentencing laws that forced judges to lock up drug offenders for long prison terms regardless of the individual circumstances or whether prison time would fix the problem.

Three-strike laws resulted in stiff penalties for a third violation of certain laws. In the case of drugs, that meant people could face the same tough sentence for smoking a joint as for selling large amounts of heroin. The disparities continue today. In some places, marijuana is legal; in some places, using it means a small fine; and in other jurisdictions, it can put you in prison for a long time. For all the mishmash, one thing is clear: about half of the inmates in federal prisons today are locked up for some type of drug offense. In state prisons, the percentage of drug offenders is much lower at 20 percent, but that's still more than for any other offense. In short, drug crimes are cramming prisons and jails.

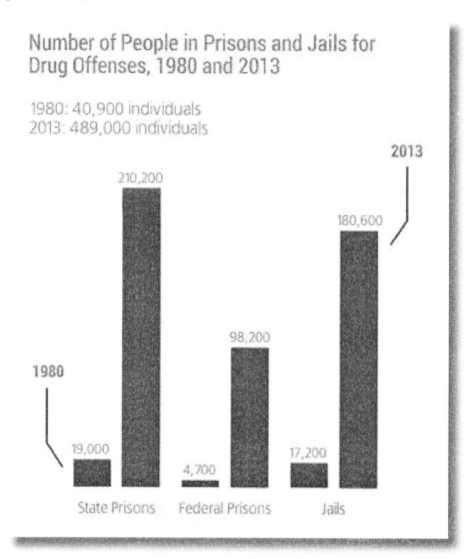

And black people are much more likely than whites to wind up behind bars because of drug crimes. Black people account for about 14 percent of our country's drug users—about the same as their share of the population—but represent 37 percent of the drug arrests and 56 percent of prisoners locked up for drug-related charges.[27] People of color also receive longer sentences than whites for drug offenses.

It sure seems like police departments and prosecutors are trying a lot harder to put black people behind bars than to lock up white people. At the very least, they seem to focus enforcement efforts where black people live. Even with a black man in the White House, some things don't seem to change.

Leaving race aside, though, **the bottom line is that drugs put people in jail, make them harder to deal with once imprisoned, and corrupt the prison system by bringing drug dealing from the street to the inside of penal institutions.**

It wasn't always this way.

In the 1950s, when I worked at the Tombs, the drug scene was very different. At first, it wasn't much of a problem at all. We saw more drunks than drug users in my earliest years as a correctional officer. By the end of my time at the Tombs in 1962, the number of drug users in jail had climbed sharply. By the time I retired, handling prisoners who were involved with drugs in one way or another was one of the toughest challenges we faced. As I've said, if it happens on the outside, it will happen on the inside, too. No matter how hard we worked at it when I was a correctional officer, we couldn't wall off the institution from drugs. From everything I know and every person I've talked to, drugs are an even bigger challenge today.

For me, the challenge of drugs in jail started at the Tombs. In the early 1960s, we began to get a lot more prisoners who were involved with drugs.

---

27 American Civil Liberties Union, "Smart Reform is Possible," August 2011, https://www.aclu.org/files/assets/smartreformispossible.pdf.

Generally, that meant heroin. Most of those who came in were users, plain old junkies whom the cops rousted in hopes they would rat on their dealers. That way, the police could go for higher-ups in the drug hierarchy. Sometimes, the strategy worked.

Whether the police started working harder at breaking up the drug trade or whether drugs just got more popular, I can't say. But suddenly, we had so many addicts coming to our jail and going through withdrawal with us that we had to set up a special unit on the twelfth floor. By the luck of the draw, that was my floor. Without any new training, I was responsible for six cots that the warden set aside for addicts in withdrawal.

It was like somebody had opened the floodgates. From six beds, we went to a dozen. The number of slots for withdrawal just kept going up. Before long, everyone on the whole floor—all 240 prisoners—was either in withdrawal or, having completed the ordeal, was cleaning up the vomit of those who were.

It was miserable. Drug addicts without drugs are unhappy, and they took it out on me. They were either begging for drugs, in pain and vomiting from withdrawal, or grousing about living with those who were still sick. Cooperation with the CO seemed a strange concept among the addicts.

Other inmates I worked with understood the logic of cooperation. They saw that it might make their stays easier; they hoped it might gain them favor—or at least avoid disfavor. For inmates, as for me, cooperation was a strategy. I didn't fully trust them, and they didn't always trust me. But we could find a mutual interest in getting through each day as painlessly as possible. As a rule, the drug addicts weren't like that. They were belligerent, nasty, and rude. It didn't help matters that instead of getting medical professionals to help them through withdrawal, they got me. I was ready to give them respect, but that didn't get me much back. That was the one instance in my career in which I couldn't find a way to connect with a fair number of the inmates on my duty post. And once they got through withdrawal, just when they might begin to work with me, they were gone—transferred back to the general population to make room for the new addicts who were going to throw up on my floor. On and on and on—the cycle didn't break. It was never going to break. It flat out wore me down.

I was crabby and tired. I was stressed when I left the jail, stressed when I got home, and stressed the next morning when I woke to start the routine all over again. At home, I became ornery and impatient. It was hard to get the drug addicts to follow my rules during the day, so I tried to make my family follow my rules at night. It wasn't a good time for anybody.

Perhaps part of the reason I struggled was because I just didn't get it. Growing up, none of my friends fooled with drugs, and neither did I. I wasn't a drinking man, either. I was fit and trim. I tried to take care of my body, partly out of pride, but also to help me be better on my job. I didn't really understand why other people would abuse their bodies with drugs. I still struggle with that. Probably I was judgmental, and that made me less open to the drugged-up prisoners than I should have been.

I wanted out. I went to the warden and volunteered to work "the wheel"—going on rotation to take whatever shift was needed on a given day—in exchange for another assignment. Going on the wheel was not my idea of a good situation either. I'd been working day shifts on the twelfth floor, generally the 8:00 a.m. to 4:00 p.m. shift. That meant dinner with my family, a regular night's sleep, and a schedule that followed the sun. I loved having a day shift, but I was ready to give it up to get a break from drug users. I needed a change; my family needed a change. And I figured the prisoners needed a change, too. We weren't connecting. I'd become little more than a babysitter, and an angry and frustrated one at that. I watched the prisoners sweat, thrash, and vomit and tried to make sure they didn't die. It wasn't the job for me.

I had no doubt that I would be a better officer if I were assigned somewhere else. For the warden, having me work the wheel would give him new flexibility. Nobody wanted to work the wheel, so I figured I was helping out the warden by being the one guy who wouldn't complain about it.

His response was disappointing. I can't describe it any other way. "Yes," he said. "I can put you on the wheel."

It sounded to me like the makings of a deal until he finished his answer. "But no, I can't change your assignment. You will stay on the ninth floor."

I was shocked. I was angry. That was a loss for me all around. I would keep working with the drug addicts, but at varying shifts that would mess up my family life and disrupt my sleep cycles. I was going to be tired and even more frustrated.

I decided I needed a new place to work in order to keep my sanity. On my transfer application, I listed my top three choices as "any place," "any place," and "any place." That's how eager I was to get off the drug floor.

Eventually, I found a berth at the penitentiary at Rikers Island. As I mentioned earlier, that's where I met Warden James A. Thomas, who would turn out to be the finest man I ever worked for.

We didn't start off too well, however. Shortly after I arrived, I made the mistake of giving an honest answer when Warden Thomas asked me what I thought of his prison. "It's filthy," I told him. "The cells are disgusting.

The corridors are disgusting." He was so surprised, so angry at my answer that he almost choked on his cigar.

I was disappointed, too. I'd expected a crackerjack operation. This was New York City's main facility for holding sentenced criminals. I'd just been at a detention center where we kept things clean. I thought I was going to the big leagues, the *prison* at Rikers Island. That was the place where New York City held convicted criminals, and I expected it to be at least as good a facility as where I'd been. In fact, I thought it would be better.

But ultimately, I came to appreciate Thomas's strengths, and he came to appreciate mine. He wasn't as focused on cleanliness as I was, but he wanted an institution that ran well and where the prisoners were treated in the right way. We thought a lot alike about our responsibilities to the inmates, and Thomas gave me the leeway to do things the way I thought made sense. He went along with my experiments and tolerated my mistakes. Eventually, he made me program director, with the responsibility for organizing entertainment and other activities to engage the prisoners in ways that made the jail a better place to be. He trusted my judgment, and he had my back.

Thomas and I started to get back on track when I helped block an escape attempt. I'd only been at Rikers a short time, and I was working the midnight shift, coming in at midnight and going off at 8:00 a.m. It was a quiet shift and generally not too demanding because the inmates were asleep. We'd go around the cells and count the prisoners as they slept to make sure nobody was missing. It took a bit of judgment and pretty good eyesight. We had to look through the bars and make sure the lumps in the beds were people, not pillows under the sheets to look like inmates who weren't there.

This night, during my regular rounds, I found a long and sharp rattail file. With a bit of patience and some hard sawing, that file could eventually cut through a bar. If it sawed through enough bars, a man could climb out.

I reported my find to my senior officer, who didn't want to believe we had a problem. "It hasn't been used," he insisted after a brief examination of the file. "Forget about it." He wasn't stupid—he was just tired and guilty of the type of inertia that keeps us from seeing things in a new way because that would mess up our routines.

But he agreed that I could have two officers to help me check the barred windows that lined the cellblock along the "flat," the ground-floor open space where prisoners hung out when they weren't locked in their cells. One by one we checked the bars. I don't know how many windows there were, but the corridor was as long as a football field. That's one hundred yards of windows—a lot of work. Eventually, we found a set of bars that were sawed three-quarters of the way though but filled with putty and covered with paint to mask the mischief. We didn't find the prisoner who did it, but we didn't lose him to an escape either.

I saw drugs and the damage they did. I saw them ruin lives and make my life harder. I'm still not quite sure what to do about them, but I'm sure that filling the jails with addicts or folks whose only crime was getting high does not make a whole lot of sense. But that's just what we've been doing: lock 'em up, lock 'em up. Law and order has been good politics, and busting folks for drugs is one way to show you mean it. It doesn't solve the real problems of drugs, but it helps fill up the jails. And it makes America the top jailer in the world. That's the wrong place to lead. I'd rather be ahead in education or jobs.

I don't quarrel with locking up drug dealers, especially the violent ones. But addicts belong in treatment, not a cell. If we're going to come down on the casual user, there's got to be something more productive than jail, like some form of probation or monitored release. For the most part, the person at risk is the person who's using—not the person walking down the street. So why lock them up? Who does that help?

Fans of *Orange Is the New Black* know the story of Piper Kerman, an affluent, young suburban woman who went to prison for acting as a drug courier on a single occasion when she was young and, in this case, stupid. Yes, she broke the law; there's no question about that. But in the ten years that had passed since her youthful mistake, she'd built a productive life, held a responsible job, and wasn't a threat of any sort to anybody. It's hard to see what anybody gained by locking her behind bars.

So what do we do in a case like that? Put her in prison to prove the law is equally hard on everybody—even rich white girls from the suburbs? It would be smarter to say, "Piper, you broke the law. We can't just forget about it. So, you will spend the next two years doing community service." Why not put her to work teaching young kids in the inner city or helping out at a food bank? That would be a better use of everybody's time than spending money to feed and house her in a prison and pay somebody like me to tell her when she can go to the bathroom and when it's time for lights out. Why not make her pay restitution and put her money to good use by buying books for a library, fixing up an old house, or funding drug rehab, which would directly relate to her crime?

The same logic could apply to thousands of others who aren't a danger to public safety, have put crime behind them, or just screwed up once—and didn't deliberately hurt somebody else in the process. We ought to try to make something good from the situation. **Too often, putting folks in a correctional institution just takes something bad and makes it worse.**

Make a person serve time, and there's a chance he or she will come out more of a criminal, more of a risk to society, and less productive than when he or she went in. Like I said, there's no correction in jail, just corruption and decay. I know that many institutions have improved since I was there. But I also know it would be even better to put fewer people behind bars. A different approach to drugs will help us get there. Let's go after violent criminals while helping everybody else make smarter choices.

New York City has been working in that direction with diversion programs that keep people out of jail cells and help them get clean. The number of people in New York City jails has been cut almost in half from almost 22,000 at its peak to less than 12,000 today, The city has gotten smarter about whom it arrests and puts on trial—and it's also developing alternatives to jail for addicts and others when a cell is the wrong answer. According to the Vera Institute of Justice, "The main causes of this drop [in the prison population] were the use of 'conditional discharge' and the expansion of programs to divert drug offenders to alternatives to prison."[28]

Fewer people in jail does not mean more crime on the streets. Crime rates have fallen sharply in New York City at the same time that the number of prisoners has gone down. I don't like all of New York's policies, especially "stop and frisk," which seems to focus on black men. But even if I have some specific criticism, **New York's experience shows you don't have to overload the jails to cut crime. In fact, you can cut crime and reduce the number of folks behind bars at the same time.**

Happily, these changes aren't just happening in New York. The US Justice Department is working to reverse national policy on drugs by giving judges more flexibility to match sentences to crimes and being pickier about whom to prosecute. It has the support of governors and senators from both parties, so maybe it will actually happen. The idea is to focus on violent criminals and drug kingpins while going easier on nonviolent offenders.

"Widespread incarceration at the federal, state, and local levels is both ineffective and unsustainable. It imposes a significant economic burden—totaling $80 billion in 2010 alone—and it comes with human and moral costs that are impossible to calculate," Eric Holder has said.

---

28 Op. Cit. NYC—Mass Incarceration Study, p. 32.

"Too many Americans go to too many prisons for far too long and for no truly good law enforcement reasons. We cannot simply prosecute or incarcerate our way to becoming a safer nation," Mr. Holder added.[29]

States are changing their approaches, too. According to the Pew Charitable Trusts, at least thirty states have modified drug crime penalties in the past few years, and they are making bigger distinctions between people holding drugs for personal use and those who are dealing for big money.[30]

Like New York City, states in every part of the country are cutting prison populations by replacing jail time with treatment programs. Supervised release programs are also growing in popularity for drugs and other crimes. We need to give drug offenders a second chance. It's cheaper. It's less disruptive and damaging for families, and it holds out a better chance that the offenders will be productive citizens in the long run. And there's one more reason—a very personal one for me. It will make life easier for correctional officers.

---

29 Eric Holder, remarks to American Bar Association, August 12, 2013.
30 "US Drug War Slowly Shifts Fire Away from Low-Level Users," *The Washington Post*, March 30, 2014.

CHAPTER 12

The Big Bear

We called him "the Big Bear." He was a tall, wide, burly guy. And hairy. He roared like a lion and looked like a bear. He was very powerful and very sick—in the head. You didn't have to be a doctor to know that this inmate had mental health problems. He was threatening to everyone and would throw feces on superior officers. Sometimes he was quiet. At other times, he would prowl around his cell, calling names or punching the air. If you've seen the movie *The Green Mile*, think of John Coffey, the mysterious and initially scary giant of a man imprisoned for a crime he didn't commit. The Big Bear didn't have John Coffey's magical powers, but he had the same overpowering presence, and there was an air of danger whenever he was out of his cell for a trip to the clinic or anywhere else he needed to go.

Generally, COs would treat him with firmness. The conversation was minimal and security intense. If the Big Bear had to go somewhere, he was typically in cuffs. Sometimes his legs would be chained together to make movement difficult in case he decided to express himself physically. For the COs, it was best when he was in his cell. If he decided to "go off" while locked up, at least he wouldn't put any officer at risk.

But one night, I treated the Big Bear differently, breaking all the rules.

Something in his voice moved me: "They're all afraid of me. That's why they won't let me out. That's why they won't take me to the clinic."

And it was true. In that section, a maximum security area for prisoners with mental health problems, the inmates rarely went to the clinic for their meds. Instead, the doctor came to them.

This night, though, felt different. The Black Bear was hurting more than usual. It was emotional pain, pain so evident I could almost feel it myself. My brain told me he needed out of his cell. For a few minutes, at least, he needed to feel human again. I was a captain by then and told the officer in the block, "Open the cell. Sign him out to me."

I didn't cuff him, chain him, or use restraints of any kind. I just let him walk, his arms and legs swinging free just like mine. Down the long corridor, we walked side by side to the cellblock gate. We got to the gate, and I reassured myself that this was the right thing to do. **I inhaled—a deep breath to steady my own nerves. Then I followed my gut and let him out.**

With the gate closed behind us, he spoke in a deep, rough voice.

"You and me? Just you and me?" he asked, surprised to be out of his cell at night without restraints or a gauntlet of officers.

This time, his voice worried me. I felt the pent-up anger and thought, *He's gonna take it out on me. Stupid, Roy, stupid.*

I braced myself for a blow. I plotted my strategy, watching him and imagining how he would move so I could get in a quick punch—maybe my only punch—before he picked me up and threw me ten miles.

"Right, just you and me," I said. I pointed in the direction of the clinic. "Let's go," But instead of fighting, he started walking. He walked down the long dimly lit corridor with no one else in sight. The deputy warden, my superior, the man in charge of the institution for the night, spotted us— and ducked out of sight. No questions, no reprimand. He was thinking self-preservation, as in *I'm outta here*. Or maybe he just refused to believe what he was seeing—quirky Roy out for a walk with that big, really crazy, and dangerous black bear.

Then we were back at the gate. I stopped to open it so we could back into the block. That's when he spoke again. He used a new tone, lighter and higher pitched:

"You see, Captain, I didn't cause you any trouble. Tell them. Tell them it's not necessary, all that security with me. It's not necessary."

He was just a big man in pain. He just wanted to feel human and be treated like any other man.

I'm a small man. I always wanted to be bigger. But this big, big man was tired of scaring people because he was so big. That was something to think about.

But I couldn't change the way we were. I couldn't make myself bigger. The Big Bear couldn't be smaller. And I couldn't keep others from seeing the Big Bear through their own eyes and being scared.

"I'm sorry," I told him softly, trying to be kind. "I can't do that. I'm just a captain. I don't make the rules. This was just me tonight, making my own moves. Just you and me. I can't make the others be like me."

And that was that.

I see now that I was negligent. Not for letting the Big Bear walk free, but for leaving it at that. I could have followed up and created an opportunity to do more. I could have found out who this man was, and why he was here. Was there a family that cared? Perhaps I could have found a way to change his life. Instead, I just went back to work. Fifty years later, that's one of my regrets.

Not that following up would have addressed the larger questions about jail and the mentally ill. Even if I had followed up and managed to improve life for the Big Bear, that wouldn't have helped the other inmates with mental health troubles of their own. Jail wasn't the best place for people with mental illnesses, but that's where they were. I couldn't change that.

At Rikers, we gave these men medication and, perhaps, some time with a therapist. But we couldn't give them the long-term attention it takes for an individual to overcome mental illness. A mental health problem usually takes months or years to resolve. For many people, such illnesses are chronic, long-term challenges that are managed or controlled but not cured. A penal institution is not the place where someone with a mental illness is likely to get better. But instead of offering the long-term help required, our country has been doing the opposite. We've cut back the number of mental health facilities, and we've been putting more and more sick people in jail instead. Between 2005 and 2010, states cut the number of psychiatric beds by 14 percent.[31] In 1955, there was about one mental health bed for every three hundred Americans. Today, there's about one bed for every three thousand.[32]

More than half of the people in jail or prison in the United States have been diagnosed with a mental illness at some point in their lives. About one in five inmates in a prison or jail has had a mental problem within the past year.[33]

It's estimated that more than 350,000 inmates suffer from "severe" mental illness. But there are only about 35,000 patients in state psychiatric hospitals. In other words, there are ten times as many mentally ill people in

---

31 "No Room at the Inn," Treatment Advocacy Center, July 2012, http://tacreports.org/storage/documents/no_room_at_the_inn-2012.pdf.
32 "Inside a Mental Hospital Called Jail," by Nicholas Kristof, *The New York Times*, Feb 8, 2014.
33 US Bureau of Justice Statistics, "Mental Health Problems of Prison and Jail Inmates," 2006.

penal institutions than in the specialized hospitals designed to treat them. The decline in hospitals is partly because over the past fifty years, we've made it much harder to commit people involuntarily. The idea is to protect people from being institutionalized when it isn't truly necessary. Instead, we wind up putting them in prison or jail—a much nastier place. A hospital, at least, might help them get better. A prison or jail is more likely to mean pain, neglect, and abuse. That's going backward.

It's a hard problem to solve, and I sure don't have the answer. There is a wide range of mental illnesses, and most of the people who struggle with their mental health aren't a threat to others. Dealing with their own lives is the more difficult part. On the other hand, people with some types of mental problems *are* more likely to break the law and more likely to commit violent crimes. Once in jail, they are more likely to cause disruption and get in fights than inmates who are mentally fit. In state prisons, for example, one of every five mentally ill inmates gets hurt in a fight. That's twice as many as those who don't have a mental health condition.[34]

For correctional officers, that means more Big Bears—prisoners who can erupt without warning or reason, battling with other prisoners, attacking officers, injuring themselves, and adding stress for everybody in the institution. In New York City, the percentage of inmates with a mental illness climbed from 20 percent to 40 percent between 2006 and 2014. Two-thirds of rules violations in the city jails are by people who have been diagnosed with a mental illness.[35]

Prisoners with mental health problems may not fully control their own actions or intend to cause trouble, but they do. But put them in jail, and they are just in the wrong place and getting the wrong kind of

---

34 Ibid. BJS, p. 68.
35 "Rikers Island Struggles With a Surge in Violence and Mental Illness," *The New York Times*, March 18, 2014.

attention. Bandy X. Lee, a psychiatry professor at Yale who studies prison violence, has explained it this way:

> "Jails and prisons are grappling with a population they are not prepared to deal with. It is not so much fault on the part of the correction system. They are simply not equipped and have not been able to adjust quickly enough."[36]

Inmates with mental illness need care from psychiatrists, psychologists, and other specialists. Instead, they are directed, disciplined, and managed by correctional officers, who no matter how well intentioned lack the knowledge and training to consistently do the right thing. Sometimes inmates die because of it.

Two recent incidents at Rikers Island illustrate the challenges. In February 2014, New York police arrested a homeless ex-marine with a history of mental health problems and charged him with trespassing because they found him sleeping under a stairwell. He was sent to Rikers, where a week later he was found dead in his cell—the victim of neglect after temperatures rose to one hundred degrees for several hours and the correctional officer on duty failed to make his rounds. The temperature in the dead man's cell rose to a life-ending level, and nobody noticed or acted until after he was dead.[37]

A year earlier, an inmate in a solitary confinement area for mentally ill inmates died after swallowing a soap ball that he'd been given so he could clean up after a toilet overflowed. The inmate, who had bipolar disorder, apparently didn't understand what the soap ball was or what he was supposed to do with it.

Unlike the homeless marine, this man had been charged with serious crimes and was awaiting trial for burglary and robbery. Like many mentally

---

36 Ibid. *The New York Times*, p. 68.
37 "Correction Department Investigating Death of Inmate at Rikers Island," *The New York Times*, March 19, 2014.

ill prisoners, he was a troublemaker for the COs, and he'd been separated from the regular population because of his disruptive behavior. But none of that excuses what happened to him. For some reason, a senior correctional officer apparently ignored reports from a junior officer that the inmate was sick and needed medical attention.[38] I hate to say this, but when the inmate is a mentally ill troublemaker, some officers just don't care.

Instead of helping the mentally ill lead better lives, locking them in jail creates a dangerous cycle of crime, prison, release, and more crime. Some individuals with mental health issues are clearly potential threats to the rest of us. But identifying these individuals and figuring out what to do about them is a puzzle we haven't mastered. Depending on the nature of their illnesses, some who commit crimes probably do belong in a correctional institution. But unless we can provide effective treatment at the same time we lock them up, imprisonment may be just a short-term interruption in the risks they pose to others.

For those who are nonviolent and whose crimes are due to mental health issues, spending time behind bars may be the least effective approach we can come up with. It we want to help the mentally ill, keep our prisons more orderly, and also keep the rest of us safe, we need to think harder. We need to figure out when mental illness is a legitimate defense and when it is not. If a man commits a violent crime because he's mentally ill, I don't want him walking free down my street—unless his illness is under control. **But a mentally ill man who sleeps in the park isn't a criminal. He needs help, not punishment.** The goal should be healing, not jailing. The truly dangerous and violent should be confined in some way. But we need to come up with the right form of confinement to create safety for the long run.

---

[38] "Complaint by Fired Correction Officer Adds Details About a Death At Rikers Island," *The New York Times,* March 25, 2014.

Perhaps we can find ways to combine time in prison with effective treatment programs. Or maybe we can place some troubled individuals in noncorrectional medical programs that help them get better. That would cut crime, reduce the load on our jails and prisons, help the troubled individuals live happier lives, and reduce the chance they will return to prison for new crimes after they are released. Locking them up hasn't worked. That just makes jails and prisons even meaner places than they need to be. We need to find a better way to deal with all the Big Bears, ease their pain, and make the rest of us safer.

CHAPTER 13

A Good Officer: What It Takes

I'm retired now, with time to think about how to fix problems with prisons and jails. But as an officer, you have to deal with the way things are and the inmates you're in charge of. What does it take to be good at the job and run the place smoothly?

As a CO, you have a lot of power. Inmates depend on you like nobody else in their lives. You tell them when to get up, when to eat, when to go to bed. They can't even get toilet paper unless you give it to them. Who else has that kind of power? Use it right, and the jail runs better. Give the inmates a fair shake, make them feel like you care, and they may even learn from your example to do better after they leave jail. And if you can't make them better people, you want to at least be sure they aren't worse than when they came in.

A good correctional officer is:

- Alert
- Proactive
- Decisive

COs always, always need to be alert, their eyes open for signs of trouble ahead and inmates who cause it. I treated inmates with respect,

but I wasn't naive. As a group, they weren't role models of good living. A lot of them were flat-out bad people.

I never trusted the inmate clerks—prisoners who helped out by checking in new inmates and directing them to their cells. They would help officers with the paperwork and recording the counts. That's a coveted job for an inmate. It gets him close to a CO and buys him a bit more freedom and a bit of protection, too. After all, why would one CO want to mess with another officer's clerk? The inmates are unlikely to bother him either. That would be like going after the teacher's pet; it's bound to get you in trouble. If the clerk's a fair-minded guy, he can make things easier for a new inmate by telling him how things work and what he has to do to get by.

But they're not always good. A new guy would come in, and the clerk might see a chance to take advantage. "Hey, you're from my neighborhood," the clerk might tell the new guy. "We're homies. I'll look out for you, so you won't have any trouble."

A day or so later, the clerk would ask, "How you doin'? Everything good?" He'd be all nice and friendly for a while, just somebody from the neighborhood looking out for a buddy. Then suddenly it would be payoff time. "You're gonna be my girl," he'd tell his homie. "You're gonna give it up to me—or I'm gonna tell everybody you're willing to give it up, and they'll be all over you, lining up at your cell."

We'd stop that once we found out, but COs can't be everywhere. We'd often need a tip or a word from the victim—if he could find a way to tell us when the other inmates weren't watching. And the truth was that most inmates didn't snitch.

If you've seen the movie *The Shawshank Redemption*, you'll recall that the Andy Dufresne character played by Tim Robbins never asked the officers for help even when sexually assaulted. Like most inmates in real life, he fought off his attackers as long as he could, but otherwise he suffered in silence.

I distrusted the clerks most of all, keeping my eyes on them like white on rice. Yes, I selected my own clerk, and I relied on him to help me out. But that doesn't mean I trusted him. We'd get along fine on the surface. But I was always watching, testing. I didn't know if he was innocent or guilty of the charges that put him in jail. But given our circumstances, I assumed he was capable of bad things.

For example, I would leave these orders with the clerk when I'd get my days off: "New inmates get the next available cell, unless I say otherwise." I didn't want any finagling or any deals to put a new man next to a prisoner who was looking for a sex partner or victim. First thing when I got back, I'd look to see if anybody new came in and where they'd been assigned. I didn't wait for the clerks to do something wrong and fix it. I stayed alert for games and tried to beat them to the punch, cutting off any shenanigans before they happened.

It's no secret that rape can be a problem in jail. I can't say how often it happened or whether it's a problem that's gotten better or worse since I retired. Rapes happen in the shadows, and nobody's going around with a tally sheet. So you have to know where they might happen and try and make them less likely. Sometimes, though, the institution makes the problem worse.

After Rikers became a detention center, headquarters realized we didn't have enough showers. The Department of Corrections decided to fix that by building new bathrooms and showers just off the dayrooms—central areas where the inmates could hang out, play cards, or just sit and talk. It was a good idea, but badly executed. The new shower rooms didn't have enough ventilation. The steam from the hot showers had nowhere to go, and in a matter of minutes the fog was so thick you could barely see your hand in front of your face. A lot of inmates simply wouldn't go into those showers. They couldn't see who might be coming up behind for an assault, and the officers couldn't see through the fog to see what was going on.

Being alert means looking out for prisoners' welfare to see when they might be in trouble. When I was working with the drug addicts at the Tombs, I noticed that one of the inmates hadn't eaten for several days and was very weak. When the doctor came to the cell block to dispense medicine, one inmate had to be carried from his section over to where the doctor was standing. Without even looking at the inmate, the doctor handed him two pills. The inmate was then carried back to his section. I approached the doctor and told him I'd appreciate it if he would take a good look at that last inmate he had just given the two pills to. I told him that the inmate hadn't eaten in two days. The inmate was then carried back over to the doctor for further examination. After the doctor put the stethoscope to the inmate's chest, he immediately ran over to me and said "he's dying". "Get an ambulance! Get an ambulance!" the doc called out. "Let's get this man to a hospital." Later, the inmate thanked me for saving his life.

Of course, being alert doesn't make a whole lot of difference unless you follow up with actions. It doesn't help to smell smoke if you don't do anything about the fire. In other words, a good CO has to be decisive. If a CO wants to keep inmates under control, he has to make it clear that he is *in charge*. That means taking action.

What I call the "Steam Table Incident" is one example. I was working in the mess hall as a supervisory officer while the inmates from our homicide cell block were being fed. The routine was simple: an escort officer would bring small groups of prisoners, perhaps thirty men, from their cellblocks to the dining room. The inmates would line up for trays and silverware under the eyes of a second officer to make sure they didn't take extra spoons to turn into weapons. After the meal, this same officer would watch the prisoners drop the used silverware into a collection bin so it could be washed. Naturally, we didn't want utensils going back to the cellblocks, so we needed to account for each piece.

The inmates would then pick up their food cafeteria-style as if they were in any one of the thousands of cafeterias on the outside. They would take the food and stand by a table until a seating officer told them to sit down. The routine made it easier to keep track of what was going on and also to make sure everybody in the group finished eating at about the same time so that we could move groups through the mess hall efficiently. We needed to get everybody fed and back to their blocks for the next count.

This day was just another routine lunch, until it wasn't. Without warning, a prisoner who had been on his way out of the mess hall bolted from the line and into the kitchen. One of my officers ran behind to stop whatever mayhem the inmate had in mind. You don't want to leave any officer on his own in that situation, so I started running to assist. The seating officer also lit out for the kitchen to find the first officer trying to separate two inmates, one of whom was stabbing an inmate, who was a kitchen worker, with a sharp handmade weapon. The other inmate was bleeding badly after being stabbed. With three officers in the kitchen, the two inmates made a break—right into the arms of other officers who had raced from their posts to help out.

We had retaken control of the fighters, but with all of those officers in the kitchen, none of us were watching the diners in the mess hall. The inmates had forgotten all about food. They were up and moving towards the kitchen, in one big mass, to see what was going on. They were energized now, they had metal utensils that could become weapons, and they were unsupervised. Responding to the first danger had potentially created a second one.

Fast as I could, I reversed course and sprinted back to retake control of the dining hall that I was supposed to be supervising. I shouted for the prisoners to sit back down, but I was talking to the wind. They kept on coming, surging forward to the kitchen—and the large knives and cooking tools inside. My words were meaningless. I needed another strategy, and fast. Without time for analysis or to consider risk versus reward, I jumped up on the big steam table that we used to keep food warm. The table was a natural barrier that protected the kitchen from the inmates, a small defensive wall where I could make a stand. **I grabbed a large steel serving spoon, raised it over my head, and warned that any man I could reach was in for it. "First man who tries to come across this table will have a goddamned busted head!"**

Maybe they thought I was crazy. Maybe they didn't want to be the first one to get smacked. Whatever the reason, they froze. They could have overwhelmed me if they just kept coming. But I'd gone on offense and changed the dynamics. In the face of decisive action, they just went back to their tables and sat down.

I can't say that the way I stopped that mob made sense—I was badly outnumbered. If they kept coming, I couldn't have hit more than one or two before I was brushed aside. But by acting fast and with firmness, I was able to take back control. It turned out to be the right move. I even got a commendation for "intelligent performance."

DEPARTMENT OF CORRECTION
CITY OF NEW YORK

OFFICE OF THE COMMISSIONER

GENERAL ORDERS NO. 10

To: ALL MEMBERS OF THE DEPARTMENT

June 16, 1971

DEPARTMENTAL RECOGNITION

Departmental Recognition is awarded to Captain Roy Caldwood, Shield No. 285, presently assigned to the New York City Adolescent Remand Shelter.

COMMENDATION

At about 10:25 A.M., March 2, 1969 Captain Roy Caldwood, who was supervising the feeding of inmates in the East Mess Hall, upon hearing an apparent disturbance occurring in the West Mess Hall, immediately proceeded to that area to investigate. Captain Caldwood, upon observing Correction Officer Eugene Fraher attempting to separate two inmates, one of whom had a knife in his hand, proceeded with Correction Officer Salvatore Portillo behind the steam table to assist Officer Fraher. As they approached both inmates ran out of the West Mess Hall where they were apprehended by other personnel. At this time, Captain Caldwood observed a large number of inmates, who were eating in the mess hall, begin to rise from their seats and approach the steam table area. Captain Caldwood ordered the inmates back to their tables. When the inmates refused to obey his order, Captain Caldwood was forced to threaten them with a large spoon he had picked up from the steam table. The inmates then returned to their tables enabling Captain Caldwood to investigate the incident between the two inmates. Said investigation indicated that as a result of an argument, inmate Pavlo Torres severely stabbed inmate Kenneth Moore with a kitchen knife necessitating the transfer of inmate Moore to Bellevue Hospital for medical treatment.

In accordance with a recommendation made by the Committee on Personnel, the Department Commendation Award, prescribed in Rule 5.70 of the Departmental Rules and Regulations, is awarded to Captain Roy Caldwood for his intelligent performance in the line of duty in this incident involving grave personal danger.

GEORGE F. MC GRATH
Commissioner

GFMcG/bn

Roy Caldwood – Commendation from Commissioner McGrath

But you can't only watch for danger. You want to spot positive opportunities, too—ways to make things better. If I could find a way to make folks smile instead of scowl, some way to lighten the weight, the place would run more smoothly and the inmates would be less likely to explode.

We always had volunteers from outside who were trying to help the prisoners turn their lives around. Some came in and taught skills like reading and writing. Others tried to help prisoners prepare for jobs on the outside. Some listened to problems and offered advice and sympathy. One of the volunteers, I discovered, was a DJ who played the latest tunes on a radio show and helped decide what music was hot and what music was not. I thought, *Why can't he do that in here?*

This was long before the Walkman and iPod, and long before music streamed over the Internet. And even if it hadn't been, the inmates probably wouldn't have been allowed to enjoy the new technology. Back then, even radios were out of reach for most. Some institutions played music in the background throughout the day; elevator music, I suppose. But headquarters didn't have much musical imagination. It ruled that only classical music was allowed something soft to keep the men calm. None of the rock, bebop, or jazz they might like but that somebody at headquarters thought might rile them up.

With the approval of the warden (a CO can't just do this type of thing on his own), I talked to the DJ and asked him if he could come back and "travel" the jail. I wanted him to bring in his equipment, move from cellblock to cellblock, and play the music the men would want to hear. I wanted him to bring in the platters and tunes he was playing on the outside and spin them on the inside. If it made the prisoners feel better and the officers relax, for a few hours at least, Rikers could be a more peaceful place to be.

And there were other ways to be proactive. I've talked about the value of prison jobs to cut boredom and give prisoners feelings of self-worth. Much as they might grouse about the work I assigned, I am certain they were happier with a "job," even one I created and even though it wasn't really within the rules. I was sure then and am sure now that working is better than sitting on your behind and twiddling your thumbs. So I came up with things for them to do.

The assignment might be as simple as scrubbing cups—tin coffee cups that were standard equipment at the Tombs. I'd get them some steel wool and set them to scouring five cups at a time, rubbing that metal until it gleamed. It kept them busy for a small part of the day; it was a way to pass some time, and we had clean cups for the mess hall. The only problem was that the prisoners weren't supposed to be assigned jobs in a detention center, and when they did have jobs, they were supposed to be paid. I was breaking the rules. One day, while a group of my inmates sat at a table scrubbing away, the commissioner of corrections happened to catch us.

Her name was Anna Kross, a remarkable woman who held New York City's top corrections post for twelve years. She was born in Russia, came to the United States as a little girl, and earned a law degree by the time she was nineteen. The second woman to be appointed correction commissioner, she was given her post by Mayor Robert Wagner in 1954 after more than twenty years as a New York City judge.

Ms. Kross was a tiny woman, barely five feet tall and with thick, thick glasses. But she also was hands-on and tough, and likely to show up at one of the city's jails or prisons at almost any time without notice to see for herself exactly what was going on. She was always looking for ways to make the institutions a bit more livable. She heard what the inmates said, and on more than one occasion, she quizzed me about their complaints. She wanted to know, "Was it good for the prisoners?" If you gave her a good answer, it was OK. On this day, she'd heard inmates on my floor complaining they didn't get enough recreation, and she wanted to know why not. I explained, "Commissioner, that is right, they aren't getting out for recreation. The inmates you heard from are on the ninth floor, where they are sent because they have drug problems. We are getting them off the drugs. Once they are finished with withdrawal, and the doctor signs off, they go back with the rest of the population and get the same chance to get recreation as everybody else." And she was OK with that.

She wanted to fix things, not just lock people away. In her final annual report (a 750-page review of her twelve years on the job), she noted that there were many types of prisoners, such as addicts and the mentally ill, "who do not belong in prison, but should be treated in a therapeutic facility."[39] Her level of personal involvement set her apart from the other commissioners I served. She was the best during my career.

But on this day, when I looked up to see her watching me and my prisoners, I thought I was in trouble. What if the commissioner didn't like my unofficial work detail? It was my first experience with Commissioner Kross, and I figured I needed a damn good explanation, or at least a fast one. Before she could quiz me, I snapped to attention and announced to her that I wanted to introduce "my VOLUNTEERS." I'm not sure she believed me about the volunteering, but she let the moment pass, and we went back to our chores. I am pretty sure I saw a slight, knowing smile on the commissioner's face, and I was certainly relieved when she kept walking down the corridor to finish her inspection tour.

---

39   City of New York, Department of Correction, "Twelve Years of Progress Through Crisis: 1954–1966," Anna M. Kross, http://www.correctionhistory.org/html/chronicl/progressthrucrisis/html/progressthrucrisis004.html.

CHAPTER 14

The Black Panthers and Other Tests

COs are always being tested. It's the nature of the job. Prisoners are always probing to see what they can get away with and what behavior will piss you off. After a few years on the job, I knew what I expected from the inmates—what I insisted on, actually. They had to keep their cells clean; they had to respect me and other officers; and they also had to respect their fellow inmates—they couldn't steal from other prisoners, or hit them, or do things to make their lives tougher. That last part was critical because jail is just like on the outside: some guys are stronger than others. They will take over and boss the other inmates around—unless the COs stopped them early on. I'd always look for those guys and try to set them straight. And, for the most part, when they saw I was serious, they would go along.

I listened to inmates' problems and suggestions and tried to fix things when I could. I had to find ways to show them I cared, and sometimes I bent the rules to make a point. When the first televisions arrived in cellblocks at Rikers, the inmates were awfully excited. They would have a new type of entertainment, a chance to watch sports, movies, music, or whatever other programs they agreed on. But we didn't have a place for them to sit. They were all standing up to watch the TV, which didn't seem very relaxing, so I told them we needed to liberate some benches. I took a few men to the auditorium, and we moved some of the benches up to the cellblock. Nobody noticed at first, but when the next Sunday rolled around and church services were held in the auditorium, there was an obvious shortage of pews.

Warden Thomas let it slide, though he had to know I made it happen, because the inmates couldn't have gone to the auditorium unless I let them in. **It was a small way I could help them out, and the inmates saw that I would take a risk on their behalf.**

At other times, though, I was so stressed that I might tell them, "Not now," "Give me till tomorrow," or, "After the weekend, 'cause right now, I don't have the patience to treat you right." By the end of most weeks, I was just too worn down to listen. Getting the weekend off, spending time with my family, and perhaps visiting a bit of land I had upstate was my chance to recover.

I remember one time in particular when it all just got to me. I'm not proud of it, but I lost my cool and punched an inmate in the face. I was working at the Tombs, and one inmate was so disrespectful and so mouthy I decided to put him on report. I didn't like to bring charges. Frankly, it was too much bureaucracy and hassle. By the time there was any official discipline, the incident was usually long past. The inmate may have even moved on to another institution or been released back to the streets. I preferred to find other ways to work it out.

I told my captain that this inmate was over the line and I was going to go by the book and write him up on charges, which usually meant a trip to solitary. The captain came up with the assistant deputy warden to see what was going on. They took the guy into the kitchen, just a few feet from my desk, and I heard this guy giving them even more lip and more sass than he had just given me. I lost it. I got up from my desk and walked into the kitchen, and from all the way down on the floor I brought my right hand smack into his jaw—right in front of two senior officers. Then I turned and went back to my post, thinking to myself, *Oh my God, Roy, what did you do? You're not supposed to hit these guys, and you did it in front of your captain. You're stupid, Roy. They're gonna get you for this. This could mean your job.*

I went back to my desk wondering how I was going to get out of this. I was yanked back to the moment by a body hitting the floor. The inmate had just landed at my feet. Apparently, the captain and the deputy had run out of patience, too. They had picked the guy up and literally tossed him out of there! That was one time I was tested and failed. Sometimes, the CO you have to watch out for is yourself.

But more often, it was the prisoners that put me to the test. Let me tell you about the Black Panthers, how they tried to stare me down, and how we ended up with a workable understanding of how things were going to be.

This was at Rikers in the early 1970s. I was program director by then, but Warden Thomas told me he had a special assignment: to oversee a group of Black Panthers who were being transferred from the Tombs, where they had caused all sorts of trouble. He didn't want trouble from them in his jail.

The Panthers were front-page news at that time around the country and had been in a number of controversial shoot-outs with police officers. They talked about promoting black pride, a cause I certainly sympathized with. They had a reputation for being tough and fearless, which was also admirable when put to good use. But I didn't think much of the way they went about reaching their goals, and I certainly didn't see how getting in gun battles was going to make life better for black Americans.

But their ideas and methods were really beside the point to me as an officer. To me, they were a management challenge—one more group of inmates that I needed to make understand that I was going to be in charge.

They came in with an attitude, thinking they could set their own rules for what they could and couldn't do at Rikers. They had an air about them: "We are THE PANTHERS. Nobody messes with us."

When they first arrived from the Tombs, they even tried to intimidate the warden, who brought the group's leaders into his office to discuss how things were going to be.

He had me bring the Panthers up from the cellblock and into his office, where he was enjoying a big cigar. The number-one Panther was very blunt about his ideas, telling Warden Thomas, "We are going to take over your institution, and when we do, we are going to lop off your head."

Thomas exploded out of his chair, chasing them out of his office and telling me to set them straight.

In big ways and small, they tested to see if I would bend to their whims or stand up to them.

The first request was about dining. They wanted to be the first in line for food and not wait behind the other inmates in the block. "We don't want to eat last. We want to eat first," they told me. I went along. But what I knew, and what they hadn't figured out, was that when you eat first, you tend to get less food. We tightly controlled the amount of food available in the early part of the mess hour to make sure the food lasted until everybody had a turn. Once the Panthers saw that the inmates at the end of the line could usually have seconds, and sometimes thirds, they had a new preference. "We want to eat last" was their new demand.

I told them no more games: "This is the last time we change the schedule. I can have you eat last, but this isn't a merry-go-round. This is the last change. The rest of the time you are here, whatever we decide now is how it's going to be."

We had a big face-off about karate and the martial arts drill they would do together in the back of the cellblock. In the warden's mind, those drills weren't just about getting exercise—they were a way to intimidate other inmates, to let them know that the Panthers could be dangerous and to do as they say. Warden Thomas told me to put a stop to it. He wasn't going to have any group of inmates trying to ride herd over others.

I couldn't just write them a note and pin it on their cell doors. If I was going to stop the karate, I had to show up while they were doing it and tell them to knock it off. I went looking to break the news. Way down at the end of the cellblock, the Panthers and a few non-Panthers who'd been transferred with them from the Tombs were doing the drills. The commands and grunts were loud enough to be heard halfway down the block. I followed my eyes and my ears to where they were.

They were arranged in formation, arms and legs thrusting forward and back with each drill. I walked along the edge of their line so that their fists nearly grazed my jaw. I could feel the wind from their high-kicking feet, which stopped just short of my chest. I walked slowly among them. Then they broke ranks to form a close circle around me. With hands going up and down, the Panthers and their friends drew in tight, screaming, "Kill, kill, kill." When they paused the screaming to catch their breath, I explained the situation:

"This is childish nonsense. This is not a movie. There are no cameras here. Cut this shit out."

"And if we don't?" one of them asked.

"Not a problem," I said. "I will just lock you in your goddamned cell, and that's where you'll stay."

I turned to leave when one of them picked up a chair. He held it high up in the air and warned, "I'm going to bounce this off your head."

"Don't tell me what you are going to do. If you want to die, throw the chair. If you have a death wish, throw the chair," I answered back.

What were they going to do? Where were they going to go? They were like rats in a trap. I wasn't making an idle threat, and they knew it. If I ordered them to go to their cells and they said no, I could bring a force of officers to put them there. And there was a good chance that at least some of those officers, who didn't like the Panthers' attitude, would be extremely forceful. It might not follow policy, but some of these COs would welcome an excuse to hit some Panthers. If I got busted with a chair, it might be even worse. For all their bluster and attitude, the Panthers understood that going along was in their own self-interest. There was a line they were unlikely to cross.

Using force wasn't my style, but the threat of force standing behind my words certainly helped keep inmates under control. I wasn't ashamed to have that weapon in my pocket and take advantage of it when I could. If inmates believed they might be hurt, they would generally follow orders to avoid it. In this way, the Panthers were like just about everybody else in jail.

There were a few more incidents after that. One day, walking through the cellblock, a couple of the Panthers were standing in my path. There was just enough space for me to walk between them. When they spotted me approaching, they stepped toward each other, closing the space with their shoulders almost touching. Their idea was to make me stop and walk around them, a kind of deference that was important to them, but that I did not want to give.

As I neared them, I stopped for a moment and moved back slightly as if to change direction. They relaxed, and that gave me my chance.

Instead of a detour around them, I stepped forward as fast as I could—but with my arms and hands together at the center of my chest. And as I stepped forward, I flung out my elbows into their shoulders with all my might. *Bam.* They weren't ready and hadn't braced for a blow, and they went tumbling—one to the right, and one to the left.

No pause, no talking. I just kept moving forward, my muscles taut in case they came after me. Five steps, ten steps, fifteen. Nothing happened. I turned to look. They were off the ground now, still surprised and staring at this crazy little CO who came up just to their shoulders. Then one of them started snorting like a bull. He walked toward me briskly, pounding his fist in his hand like he was going to commit mayhem on my face or body. But I held my ground, feet rooted firmly in place, ready to defend myself if need be. And he just kept on going. Never touched me.

The only serious challenge after that actually came from an inmate who hung with the Panthers but wasn't actually a Panthers member. It was as direct and brazen a threat as I heard the whole time I worked in corrections.

"We can find out where you live, and we can take care of your family," he told me.

That was a helluva threat. I was seething. It was all I could do not to put my hands on his neck. I was direct: "Let me tell you guys something—you had better make sure nothing ever happens to my family," Still shaking, I walked away before I did something I would regret.

The next day, one of the Panther leaders came to me quietly, all apologies.

"Captain Caldwood, that man was out of line what he said to you. We straightened him out."

For the most part, after that, we got along fine. However, they did surprise me one more time.

Eventually, detainees move on, either back to the streets or upstate to serve their sentences. In this instance, a Panther was going upstate. He had signed a pledge to his comrades that he wouldn't rat them out when he got there, and he asked me to sign as a witness! That was one of the nuttiest ideas I'd ever heard, but it showed how much things had changed from when we started.

It's not just the prisoners who test you. Sometimes your bosses have bad ideas, and your fellow officers do things they're not supposed to do. In every workplace, people have to make choices: when you will go along, when you will turn your eyes to small infractions, and when you will say no.

COs are supposed to protect prisoners—most often from one another, but also from other COs, and sometimes from "higher authority." That's the part of my job that often caused me to say no. Once I made it to captain, I had more power to make my "no" stick.

One time at Rikers, after a fight between and inmate and an officer, I hustled from my station to see what was going on. By the time I got there, the fighting had ended, and both men had cuts and bruises. Other officers took the bruised CO to the clinic for repairs, and I took the inmate to get sewed up. After our clinic visit, I was walking him back to his cellblock, him in front and me behind. At the end of a corridor, but before getting him into the block, I opened a gate and let him go through. What I didn't see at the time was that two officers were standing just inside that gate. They were still unhappy about the fight and decided to administer further justice with their clubs. I guess they hadn't seen me. At the first blow and scream, I doubled my pace. They were swinging fast, and it doesn't take many blows to hurt a man badly. I scrambled through the gate to protect the prisoner, pulling him behind me and presenting my body as a shield. "If you want him, you have to go through me," I announced, and the beating stopped. That was the end of that. The officers seethed, but they obeyed. I was a captain. Hitting me or belting the inmate again could have cost them their jobs.

CHAPTER 15

A Snitch and an Escape Stopped

If you've watched movies or TV shows about jail, it might surprise you to know that there aren't many snitches in jail. Popular entertainment often shows inmates passing information or quietly sharing quick tidbits with the officers and getting small favors in return. Sometimes it happens, but not very often. **As a rule, there are few rats in jail. Squealing can be dangerous, and, in truth, I didn't have much to offer inmates in return.** I couldn't help them at trial, change their verdicts, or cut their sentences. The warden couldn't either. There are pretty strict rules about that.

In the rare cases that an inmate talks, there's usually a very specific reason, and it's not because he likes the CO or is looking for a favor. He might be taking revenge against another inmate—passing information that would get another guy in trouble or lead to more charges and more time. Or he might be afraid for his life and thinks squealing is the best chance to be safe. Worrying about his life was the reason an inmate once snitched to me about something big.

The information he gave me helped us foil an escape attempt from maximum security at Rikers. I doubt the inmates would have gotten far, because getting off the island would be tough even if they got out of the jail. But it was a lot easier for us to block it in advance than to track down fugitives later on.

The plan began to come undone when, by coincidence, I told one of the plot leaders that we were transferring him to the Tombs. As happened with Cuba, it was a routine transfer because his trial date was due. We weren't up to any trickery or trying to disrupt any plans—but it turned out that's exactly what we did.

The guy was in maximum security, so his charges must have been severe. But in jail he hadn't caused any trouble. He was quiet, smart, and respected—even by the COs. He wasn't confrontational and did as we asked. In that way, he was a model prisoner.

But that quiet front may have been a strategy to improve his chance of getting away. Because he didn't cause trouble, we didn't pay him much mind, and that left him a bit freer to move around as he wanted and also to work with others on a plan to escape.

When the transfer order came through, I was the guy who delivered the news. I went to the cellblock and called out, "John Johnson."

That was unusual. I probably should have been quieter, because as soon as I hollered, every eye turned to me. There were twenty-five or thirty inmates in that area, and they didn't like what was going down. Johnson himself didn't react much because that wasn't his style. By staying low-key, he probably figured there was less chance he would give anything away.

But I could sense the other inmates weren't taking it as well. He was their Moses, the man whose escape plan was going to lead them to freedom. At least that's what they were hoping for. I felt the rage and thought they were ready to hurt me. So I kept my eyes locked on Johnson rather than turn around to face their animosity. I could see him signal with his eyes to the others that they should stay cool. Silently he had waved them off because attacking me wouldn't help them. Once he did that, I felt safe enough to leave. I signaled the control room to open the gate. I walked out, through the rotunda, past the control room, and up one more flight to my office.

Soon after, an officer came to my door. He had an inmate from max security pleading for a few minutes of my time.

The inmate was red in the face, anxious, and sweaty from some kind of ordeal. It took him just a few minutes to explain.

He'd been in the back of the cellblock when I told Johnson of his transfer. The other inmates figured Johnson was being sent away because we had found out about the escape and wanted to break it up. That would mean that somebody had tipped us off, and, for some reason, they had pinned it on this inmate.

"We got a dime dropper here, and you're the rat," they told this guy.

Instead of denying it or getting angry, which might have gotten them off his back, he panicked. No sooner had they fingered him than he set off running to the front of the block where a CO might protect him or even get him out. Of course, running only made him seem guilty, and the others were hot after him to get their revenge.

He got to the gate ahead of his pursuers, but the gate was locked, and he couldn't get out. He ducked into an open cell and tried to slam the cell door shut behind him. But the other inmates were close, and he couldn't shut the gate behind. One of the other inmates came in with a knife, while the rest kept a lookout for the CO, who by then was headed their way. The suspected rat hopped up on the bed, bobbing and weaving this way and that, trying not to get stabbed.

He managed to stay out of range long enough for the officer to get to the cell, which saved the man's life because the other inmates cleared out when they saw the officer on his way.

As it ended, they told their suspect that they were just testing him to see if they could find the rat.

"Testing, hell, you were going to kill me," he snarled back.

Then he broke for the gate again, screaming for help. "Let me out, let me out," he begged. And that's what the officer did. When he got to my office, he spilled the beans.

He told me there were a homemade key and some weapons for an escape. He also told me where we could find them. We went in fast, before the inmates in the block could find new hiding places. Everything was just as my snitch said. We had the goods. We transferred Johnson as planned—and the squealer, too. It was the only way to keep him safe.

CHAPTER 16

In the Library

Keeping the prisoners' interests at the front of my mind was an effective strategy for me. I tried to put myself in their shoes and think about what would make me more cooperative if I were the one in custody. That's why I rearranged the library the way I did at Rikers without even thinking of asking for permission. I never thought it was the sort of thing that somebody might want to micromanage.

I wasn't out to make a revolution. I was just responding with common sense to a set of changing circumstances. For one thing, Judge Lasker had ordered some adjustments in the way Rikers operated. Ruling in a lawsuit about conditions at the jail, he wanted us to help prisoners with their cases by setting up a law library and bringing in a law librarian to give them help. But at about the same time that Judge Lasker was trying to make things better, a program that was paying for social workers to help inmates with various problems lost a big part of its funding.

For a brief time, there had been enough social workers that we were able to have one available in each cellblock. We'd escort them into the block, and inmates on that block could sign up to see them. It was a win-win all around. It made life easier for COs because we could manage the flow and didn't have to escort inmates in and out of the block for counseling. The inmates could get more time with a counselor because there were more of them, and because the workers would be responsible for specific cellblocks, they could see the same prisoners on a regular basis and actually get to know them a bit. That continuity built trust and made the counseling more effective. When we lost funding, however, we were suddenly down to three social workers from nearly a dozen. That meant sending the workers into the blocks wasn't going to be practical, so I thought, *What about the library?* A central and consistent location would make the program more manageable and help us maintain security. We were already making changes as we brought in law books and law librarians; maybe the social workers could set up shop there, too.

I figured I could section it off so that there would be an area for each function—regular books here, law books there, and another area for counseling. Better yet, I remembered that we had some unused "teaching booths" in storage. They were really just little two-person containers with a shelf for books or other materials, and they were closed on two sides to provide a bit of privacy. Privacy seemed like a good idea for counseling sessions and for looking at law books, too. I got permission to use those booths in the library. The inmates would wait their turn for a social worker, go into the booth for their conversation, and then give up the booth to the next guy in line. **I thought it was all working pretty well, until I ran into a guy from City Hall.**

I got a call from the warden that I was about to get visitors: one of the deputy corrections commissioners was on his way to the jail, and he was bringing another official with him, somebody who worked for Mayor Beame. Not a problem. I'd given tours for many visitors over the years. But the second guy in the twosome was in charge of all the libraries in the correctional system, and he didn't much care for the way I'd set things up.

"This has all been changed around. It's not the way we run things in New York City," he said. "This type of arrangement has been tried upstate, and it was chaos."

It felt like an ambush, and I bristled back up at him (he was about six feet four, way above my eye level).

"Well, this is working for us," I told him. "I hope I don't have to call you every time I move a couple of chairs. It that's the case, we've got a problem."

I'd put a little chill on that conversation, but they didn't say any more, and after a few days I'd forgotten the whole thing.

Then, a month or so later, my critic showed up again—this time with the mayor in tow. They had come to see a show with the prisoners. Afterward, Mr. Big Man, as I'd come to think of him, tracked me down and asked if I could show the mayor around. Of course he wanted to visit the library. He'd been checking up on me, and I thought I might be challenged in front of the mayor. When we got inside the library, I braced myself as the man began to speak.

"Mr. Mayor," he said. "Look at this library. I told Captain Caldwood it wasn't going to work the way he set it up. But my people have been checking, and they tell me it's working great. I was wrong."

You could have knocked me over with a feather. Not only hadn't he come after me, he'd gone out of his way to praise me to the top man in New York City. I ran into him again later on and told him how surprised I was—and appreciative, too.

I pride myself on reading people, but I was dead wrong about Mr. Big.

On the other hand, I could read the prisoners pretty well.

In the early 1970s, Rikers Island played host to a woman who would later become one of the FBI's most wanted fugitives. Joanne Chesimard, a member of the Black Panthers and the Black Liberation Party, was convicted of shooting and killing a New Jersey state trooper during a traffic stop in 1973. Ms. Chesimard, also known as Assata Shakur, later escaped from a New Jersey state penitentiary and fled to Cuba. In 2013, the FBI made her the first woman to appear on its list of most wanted terrorists.

For a time, she was housed in the Women's House of Detention on Rikers Island while awaiting trial for several robberies and shootings in New Jersey. In those days, COs were assigned by gender—women to the women's house, and male COs at facilities for men. So I had no contact with her until the warden told me that the courts ruled that the male Black Panthers and Joanne Chesimard should be allowed to hold a meeting.

It didn't matter to me where Ms. Chesimard and her compatriots met, so I figured I would leave the choice to the prisoners. I showed one of her codefendants the available conference rooms, starting with the best one. It had a big, long conference table, attractive photos on the wall, comfortable furniture, and good lighting. The only thing it lacked was a view.

I recommended it as the best room we had, but he rejected it. I wasn't surprised. In fact, his reaction was predictable. He figured we would bug the room and tell the prosecutors what we heard. He also figured that whatever room I showed him would have the bugs.

"No problem," I told him. "I'll show you all the rooms, and you pick the one you like."

There were about four or five, and I walked him down the corridor so he could look at each one. The other rooms simply weren't as nice. They were smaller or less comfortable, or the lighting wasn't as good. After examining and rejecting each one, he decided he liked the first one after all. And that's the one I had them use.

I'd given him the right to choose, a small bit of freedom he wasn't used to inside. And why not? We weren't bugging the rooms, and it really didn't matter to me. So why not let him have this small bit of control, if only for a few moments of one day when he could pick a meeting room? I wasn't surprised that he wound up back at the first room. It was the best room, and by letting him choose, I wore away his suspicions. When he was able to choose for himself, he assumed it was on the level because he knew we couldn't wire up every room. It would be too much time and too much money. And that made him comfortable enough to pick the one I'd recommended in the first place.

CHAPTER 17

Weddings Let in Some Light

Sometimes, good things DO happen in jail. I saw a lot of gloom and human waste, but I was also amazed at times by individuals who voluntarily came to Rikers to try to help the prisoners. They generally don't get much credit or notice, but every day when I was at Rikers, we opened the doors to volunteers who were there because they wanted to be.

At the top of the volunteer roster was Barbara Margolis. A wealthy Jewish woman who served as New York City's chief of protocol under Mayor Edward Koch, Barbara was a regular at Rikers Island for more than thirty years. She began in the 1960s with a series of programs teaching inmates about art, journalism, horticulture, and cooking. She called her initiative START: Services to Adolescents through Release of Tensions. Over the years, that program evolved into Fresh Start, which provided inmates with job training and job placement with an emphasis on restaurant work. Barbara had a group of restaurants that would hire her graduates when they got out. And their release wasn't the end of it for her. She kept in touch with her grads after they left jail. She said she wanted to "smother" them so they'd do the right things. She didn't just write checks. She rolled up her sleeves and worked at it, picking up the phone to check on former inmates personally to see how they were doing on the outside.

"She would take phone calls from [Fresh Start] graduates at ten o'clock at night. She would go to their weddings. If they needed a tie for an interview, she would get them a tie," said Jennifer Wynn, a former Fresh Start director.[40]

And her programs got results. The Osborne Association, which took over Fresh Start after Barbara retired, says that the program's graduates are only half as likely as other former inmates to wind up in jail again within a year of their release.

Barbara and the people who volunteered with her weren't unique to New York. Every day, thousands of people like her in large and small programs across the country are still trying to help prisoners with the type of programs that Barbara Margolis pioneered. And what they are doing works. With the right kind of help and their own commitment, people can get out of jail and succeed. But we need to get our priorities right. **Instead of working to put people in jail, we should be working to keep them out of jail—not by letting criminals go free, but by giving them the support to get by through honest work.**

Barbara knew what it took to "correct." She wasn't afraid to bend or break rules if that was what it took. In the 1960s and 1970s, when I knew her at Rikers, inmates weren't able to make phone calls for themselves. Instead, calls were filtered through a CO, who would talk to the inmate, make the phone call to the family or friends, write down what was said, and report it back to the inmate. Barbara often short-circuited the process, taking inmates to her office and handing them the phone.

When I was program director, she helped me start an arts program for adult inmates. Under contract with the city, Barbara worked with adolescent inmates. At that time, teen inmates were housed in their own section

---

[40] "Barbara Margolis, Prisoners' Advocate, Dies at 79," *The New York Times*, July 13, 2009.

of the Rikers House of Detention for Men. You could walk down the corridor from the adult facility to the adolescent wing. That's where I got to know her.

The arts program was a terrific idea. It provided the adolescents with a way to use their hands and brains, to be creative, and to stay out of trouble. As a new program director, I wanted to copy what Barbara had done and start one for the adults—but there wasn't money in the budget for that.

So we worked out a little scam. Eventually, the adolescents were moved to a new facility on the island. And when Barbara left the first institution, tables and chairs from there followed her to the new location. To me, that was an opportunity.

"Barbara," I said, "that furniture actually belongs to the adult jail. The warden says we should take them back. But, you know, there might be a better way to work it out. I need money for an arts program. I need to buy supplies so my men can learn just like the kids you're working with."

The corners of her mouth turned up a bit, and I could see she knew where I was going.

"But I could talk to the warden. I am pretty sure he would make a deal. If you could set up an account at the art store in Flushing, we could buy some supplies. I would send an officer to the store when we run low on supplies and charge it against the account."

She nodded and told me she would send a check for $300 to the store with full instructions for how the money could be used. That would be about $2,000 in today's money, so we could buy a pretty good amount of basic supplies. This would be the first time that I received funds to help me run a program. I was a program director without any budget and wasn't allowed to incur any overtime expenses. My recreation officers often worked without pay in order to help my programs succeed.

Barbara wasn't supposed to support adult programs, but this was a way to get around her contract and help at the same time. That's how adult men at Rikers first got a chance to test their skills at art.

Barbara's check paid another dividend by helping us get Mercer Ellington to bring his band to Rikers and play some big band swing for the inmates. The way I hooked him was a piece of inmate art: a mural of Duke Ellington, Mercer's father. Duke Ellington had just died, and I thought that Duke's family might be pleased to know that Duke had fans even in jail.

It was surprisingly easy to approach the Ellingtons. I just picked up the phone. An officer I'd worked with at the Tombs knew the family. I got the phone number from him and dialed. Mercer was on the road with the band, but I told his wife about the mural and how I hoped Mercer might come over and dedicate it. She promised he would give a call when he got home.

That might have been the end of it, but sure enough, a few days later, my phone rang, and it was Mercer Ellington. I didn't have to go through an agent or a lawyer like I might today. Mercer agreed to bring the band. So we threw a sheet over the painting and had an official unveiling. Then the band began to play. As simple as that.

We had other musicians, too. Dee Dee Bridgewater, the jazz singer who was making a big splash on Broadway, put on a show. **We had James Brown, too. He came with his singers, the Famous Flames, and a complete set of musicians—he even had a full dress rehearsal in the auditorium.** To be honest, his music wasn't my cup of tea. I liked big band dancing from when I was young. The Ellingtons were more my style, but the inmates went wild for Brown—dancing, twisting, jiving, and singing right along. There may have been an extra bond because Brown had done some time as a very young man. As I understand it, jail was where he started his first group—singing with his cellmates in Toccoa, Georgia.

I'd gotten Ellington to the jail on my own, but I was connected to Bridgewater and Brown by a group of volunteers from the Hospital Association. The group hadn't started out to help prisoners. Its job was to entertain hospital patients. I got to know its director, and she put me in touch with the entertainers that her group dealt with. So the Hospital Association became my main talent agency. It was a real godsend for me and the prisoners.

One year, some of the prisoners put on their own musical show. There's a lot of talking that goes on in jail with inmates boasting about things they did on the outside, and word gets around. Listening to the chatter, I knew that some of the inmates could play, so when I heard a few of them saying they wished they could get up a band, a lightbulb flashed. I thought that if I could rustle up some instruments, it just might be fun.

There wasn't any money to buy instruments, and prisoners couldn't just run home and get their own. But I remembered that when I worked there, the Tombs had some instruments stored away. I found out they were still there and got permission to borrow them. The women's jail on Rikers had three pianos, and the folks over there said they would lend me one—providing we put the show on for the women inmates, too. That was an easy condition to agree to.

And I got volunteer help for the show—not from outsiders, but from my fellow COs at the jail, who worked off the clock to provide security during rehearsals. We were still in jail. Even when putting together a musical show, we had to stay alert. As I've said, I always expected the unexpected. Pulling inmates together to rehearse a show can't happen without security. In fact, just about everything I did as program director was possible because I had a terrific crew of COs who were ready to help out. On television and in the newspaper, we hear about the bad things that some COs do. I don't complain about that—if we don't know about bad things, we can't fix them. But the COs at Rikers did a lot of good things, too. I'm glad to have this chance to tell about it and to say thanks to my crew.

I had good luck with our shows. The inmates didn't cause trouble or act out. Looking back, those shows might have been the safest, most peaceful times we had. The inmates could feel human again for a little bit and almost forget they were in jail. And they didn't want to do anything to get thrown out of the show—or banned from the next one. They were pretty much on their best behavior.

In fact, I'm the guy who probably enjoyed the shows the least. It was my job to make sure things ran smoothly, and I never could relax. I was always worried that something would go wrong. Putting hundreds of inmates together in a hall does that to a correctional officer. It wasn't until they were back in their cellblocks that I could let out one big sigh of relief.

And sometimes the unexpected did happen. But the problems were with the shows, not the prisoners.

One time, the Hospital Association sent us over a fashion show. I guess I had some misgivings about having pretty women parading around in front of men who were locked away from female companionship, but I decided to take a chance. What I didn't count on—or think to check on—was exactly what the models were going to wear. It turned out they didn't wear enough for my taste.

To be honest, I wasn't paying much attention to the show. I was focused on the inmates and how they were behaving. I could tolerate a few wolf whistles and catcalls, and even the occasional shout to "take it off" (though maybe I should have been more sensitive to how the models might feel). But I had my eye out for any behavior that really got out of line.

I was actually pretty oblivious until one of the inmates said, "Hey, Captain, she's not wearing any underwear!" That got my attention. I took a closer look, and darn if some of those outfits weren't see through, and sure enough I didn't see undergarments. That was too much. I ran backstage, grabbed one of my officers, and told him to be damn sure that every girl from then on was fully clothed underneath. Underpants and a bra was my bottom line.

There was another show that scared the hell out of me. One of the art groups around town came to us with a proposal for two events—a musical and a play—that they wanted to perform for the prisoners. I never had any money to pay for programs, and this group was willing to put on the shows for free. It sounded like a good deal. I figured the director was getting a dress rehearsal, and I was getting a show. **They told me the show was called *Brotherly Love*. That sounded great. What would you want more in a jail than some brotherly love?**

Then the curtain went up. On stage was a circle of black men, with one guy sitting in the middle and the others circling around like an Indian war dance from the movies. A murmur rose, and their voices slowly got louder until they broke into a rhythmic chant. Over and over, they were screaming, "Kill Whitey, kill Whitey, kill Whitey."

Oh my God, I thought, *what happened to brotherly love? This is not appropriate. I've got to get it to stop before the inmates take up the chant and maybe try to act it out.* But I also realized that a CO jumping on stage to cut it off might set them off as well.

I ran to the front row, but the director refused to intervene. "It's all fine," he assured me. But it wasn't all fine to me. I turned to my inmate MC. "Eddie," I said, "I can't have this. Can you stop it?"

He was cool. "I got it," he assured me. Just as the actors turned their backs to the audience at the end of the scene, Eddie saw his moment. He hopped on the stage, grabbed the mike, and announced, "That was terrific. Great show. Let's give them a hand." And he dropped the curtain. Maybe the inmates were as confused as I was, because they didn't protest. We took them back to their cellblocks and called it a show. I never found out what the rest of the play was about, and I still don't want to know. But that episode taught me to take a closer look at the script before agreeing to a show.

We had a little problem with our basketball league once. But, again, it wasn't because of my inmates. This time it was because of the women at the jail next door.

The basketball league was probably the most popular program I organized as program director. Think about it. We had a bunch of men who were mostly young and fit enough to play some ball. We were an urban institution. More specifically, we were in New York City, a town well known for competitive playground basketball. In a lot of neighborhoods, the most respected guy was the guy who could play some ball. And that became even more so as the jail population became blacker.

I told the prisoners that every cellblock could have a team, and that cellblocks could play each other. We weren't set up to hold tryouts, but it was the same as finding musicians. Word gets around fast about what inmates say they can do, and basketball was a favorite topic. Everybody pretty much knew who could play and who couldn't without even picking up a ball. Of course, my volunteer COs checked them all out. We got a ball and brought in the guys with the reputations to see if their skills matched the hype. Usually they did. That's how we put the teams together.

But when we took the guys over to the women's house to put on a game, things got a little bit crazy. Of course, we put them in cuffs for the trip over. Some of these guys were charged with serious crimes and facing long time. They might look for a chance to escape, and I wasn't going to make it easier just because they played basketball.

The stereotype has it that it's men who won't know how to behave, but I had laid down the law beforehand. We were going to the women's house for basketball, not a social hour. I didn't want them paying those women any mind. That could cause trouble. In the end, the women were the ones who got out of hand.

The game was officers against adolescent inmates, and the women were into it. That is, they were into the young men flashing their basketball skills and their muscles. They were fighting in the stands. Female officers were rushing to break up each fight. The women didn't keep their thoughts to themselves. They were calling out throughout the game: "Go, honey." "Ooh, like that butt." That sort of thing. Innuendo after innuendo, and come-on after come-on. When the game was over, the women wouldn't leave. Hands on hips, they said, "We ain't going nowhere."

I herded my men into the dressing room to wash up and change, and the women were outside the door. *Boom*, they broke down the damn door and started coming after my guys. I had a helluva time getting them back safely to the bus. There might have been a few winks and smiles from the men, but my inmates kept themselves pretty well in line. The women, however, were out of control. On that day, at least, that institution wasn't running the way it was supposed to.

But probably the best thing I did as a CO was to hold weddings. I helped organize three of them in 1974. And it wasn't just a case of bringing in a justice of the peace to read the vows. We turned them into real celebrations. We had music with singing by inmates who performed professionally when on the outside. I had the kitchen provide wedding cakes baked by other inmates so they could share the wedding joy, too. We couldn't have beer or wine or any other alcohol, of course, but we got some sodas for the guests.

The brides and grooms dressed up just like they would on the outside. I still have a picture of one couple in matching white suits, looking good, with a big silky white bow tie on the groom. They glowed, like brides and grooms at every wedding. One of the brides sent me a card afterward and wrote: "Years from now, when my son is born, I will tell him about you and the beautiful wedding you gave us." I got a thank-you note from a groom, who asked me to "keep doing good things for the inmates."

Those notes are among my most prized memories. They made the job worthwhile.

JUNE 20-1974

A.D.W. CALDWOOD:

Sir,

Please find enclosed a wedding picture of my wife, Vernell, and myself.

My wife and I wish to thank you for your help you gave so whole-heartedly in arrangeing for us to be wed in this institution.

I'm sorry that I could not give you this picture in person. But as you know, I had a little trouble with one of your Captains and was sent to the Bing.

The case I had in the state court, was disposed of and I was turned over to the federal people.

Kap doing good things for the inmates. Most of us need it.

Once again, "THANK YOU"

Yours Truly

Inmate Wedding Thank-you Note

CHAPTER 18

One More Riot

In 1974, I was organizing weddings. In 1975, I was trying to break up riots.

In some ways, that statement summarizes the roller coaster ride of a correctional officer. No matter how many good programs we came up with, how many weddings we celebrated, or how much effort any individual officer put in to making the place better, there were bigger forces that made things worse. New York City was in financial trouble. It was cutting costs to make ends meet, and one place it was cutting was the correctional system. The Tombs had been shut down by order of federal judge Morris Lasker because of poor conditions there, and about five hundred inmates were sent from there to Rikers. At the same time, the number of COs had been cut back. So, instead of five to a cellblock—which wasn't enough to begin with—we were down to four, and some of the blocks held more than three hundred prisoners. In February 1975, Judge Lasker said some things at Rikers were so inadequate that they violated the Constitution.[41] In short, Rikers was a very bad place to be.

The judge was 100 percent right. He didn't like the fact that the prisoners couldn't get much exercise. Gym facilities were limited. We didn't have enough COs to provide security in the outside yards. The prisoners were getting fifty minutes a week of recreation, and the judge said it should

---
41 "Judge Says Rikers Violates Rights," *The New York Times*, February 21, 1975.

be at least five hours. There were other grievances, too. Food was bad. Medical care was poor. The inmates couldn't make phone calls. We didn't allow contact visits, so the men couldn't even hug their moms or girlfriends or children when they came to visit.

The problems were well known but never seemed to get addressed. **The system just kept saying no. Instead of figuring out how to make sensible changes and still have security, it was just *no, no, no*. It should never come to a point where the only way the prisoners can be heard is by taking hostages.** But when a prisoner takes hostages, he can get the system to pay attention. So that's what happened.

It was late November 1975, less than a week before Thanksgiving. We had a new warden, Louis Graziano, who had come in a few months before. I was an assistant deputy warden by this time, which had given me a nice bump up in pay and responsibility. Because of layoffs, we were short on personnel. Working double shifts had become common for COs. On this day, I was working the 8:00 a.m. to 4:00 p.m. shift, and Warden Graziano had assigned me to stay around from 4:00 p.m. to midnight as well. It was rare for men of my rank to work doubles. It was my first double shift since I was appointed program director four years before. I didn't like it, but at the time I considered it just one of those things.

I was walking the rounds on the second half of my day, checking with the gate officers stationed outside each block to control movement in and out. The gate officer at block five was worried. He had a sense that something was in the air. There was an unusual huddle of inmates down at the end of the block—almost a hundred yards away. For the gate officer, it's like trying to figure out what play the other team's quarterback is going to call when you're way down in the opposite end zone. He hadn't heard of anything amiss from the one officer inside the block, and he couldn't leave his post to find out. But he wanted to share his suspicions and put me on alert.

With the heads up from that officer, I was prepared for trouble when I got a call from block seven that officers had found some loose bricks. The block officer had initially found a small hole in the bathroom wall, which appeared to be missing a single brick. He told his captain, and when the two of them returned for closer inspection, the hole had doubled in size and two bricks were on the floor. Just in the ten minutes or so of walking back and forth in the block, the inmates had been back in the shower area pulling out more. Standing outside block seven, they gave me their report and handed over the bricks. The hole was in an inside wall separating cellblocks. It wasn't the start of an escape hole nipped in the bud. The bricks were ammo for a fight. Unlike block five, with its massed huddle of inmates, block seven was quiet. The usual hum of inmates' chatter was strangely absent from the air. Too quiet, I thought. Something was about to blow up.

A loud, high-pitched scream from the gate officer outside block seven jolted me into a trot to the block. **Inside, all hell was breaking loose. Two officers were under attack in the block.**

"Open the gate. Open the gate," I told my gate officer, who had the key to the block. He objected. "No, no, Dep. They'll come out. They'll come out."

And he was right. Opening the gate isn't the protocol. By the book, we were supposed to keep them locked *in* the block. If we opened the gate, the inmates might get out. But there were officers in there, too. They were outnumbered. It was literally one hundred against one, and they were going to be overwhelmed, beaten, and taken. It wouldn't take long if we couldn't get them out now.

"Open the gate," I ordered again. "Open the goddamn gate!"

I was in. Both officers who were in that cell block were fighting off hoards of inmates. One office on the left and the other on the right, about forty feet diagonally across from each other. I raced up to the officer on my left, at that point the inmates turned and started running away from him. He began to run after them. I caught up to him, grabbed him by his shirt and yanked really hard. He spun around as if to fight me off too, but the uniform said I was his friend. Our eyes locked. I tugged at him. "Get out. Get out!"

He sprinted towards the exit gate. I then looked to my right to see what was happening to the other officer. The inmates who were attacking him also retreated back into their cell block. He was standing alone. He looked over to see what was happening with his fellow officer. But, instead of seeing him, he saw me. **Our eyes locked and he froze. I gestured to him to get out now. He quickly sprinted towards the exit gate. The three of us were now all out of the cell block. We slammed and locked the cell gate. There were two other officers in the rear of that cell block that I wasn't able to rescue. I sent an officer racing to the control room: "We have a riot," he reported. "The inmates have block seven."** The control room activated the standing riot plan and summoned all the officers it could find.

> **Department of Correction — Intradepartmental Memorandum**
>
> **Date:** 12/30/75
> **From:** Captain Sotirios Damaskos # 458
> **To:** A/D/w R. Caldwood H.D.M.
> **Subject:** Disturbance which occurred on Nov. 23, 1975 in the H.D.M.
>
> At appr. 8:45 PM on 11/23/75, while making my tour of 7 Block, C.O. Maloney called my attention to a ceramic brick that was missing from the wall on the "A" side shower room. After I inspected this hole in this wall, and not finding the brick, I called A/D/w Caldwood and informed him of the situation. There was no lock for the shower room door. While awaiting A/D/w Caldwood, who respond promptly, I again inspected the hole in the 7 "A" side shower room wall. The hole in the wall had increased to an area of appr. 1½' by 3'. Two bricks were lying on the floor. A/D/w Caldwood inspected the involved area, and told me to take the two bricks I found to the security office, and return to 7 Block.
>
> I brought the two bricks to the security office, and started to go back to 7 Block. When I reached 6 Block in the corridor, I saw A/D/w Caldwood leap back from the "A" gate of 7BL, and heard a crash. I ran to 7BL, and saw that the inmates had control of 7BL, and were brandishing weapons, of sticks etc. The time was appr. 9:25 PM. 11/23/75.
>
> At appr. 9:28 11/23/75 while A/D/w Caldwood and I were walking to the front of the building to mobilize the available Officers, 5 Block erupted. Two rail officers responded, and the "A" gate of 5BL was opened, in order to extricate C.O. Robinson who was clinging to the gate. The inmates were trying to pull C.O. Robinson back into the block. We got C.O. Robinson out of the block, and an inmate who was bleeding from his back, and managed to lock the "A" gate of 5BL.
>
> I then went to the security office and mobilized the available men, and to issue riot equipment.
>
> CAPT. Sotirios Damaskos # 458

Intradepartmental Memo - Inmate Disturbance

I remained standing in the corridor between cell block seven and five. Suddenly I heard that same familiar blood curdling scream that had previously come from the CO outside of block seven. I raced to block five, which was about twenty feet away, along with my captain. Looking into the cell block, we saw multiple hands on the gate. The inmates were back to belly, side by side, pressing up against the gate. It was pandemonium. I knew that someone was in a lot of trouble. I had to take action fast. I ordered the CO, that was standing next to me, to open the gate. It was a replay of block seven just moments before. "Open the gate, open the gate," I shouted at the gate officer. "No, no," he said, "they'll come out." I repeated the order, with emphasis, he unlocked the gate. All hands came off of the gate. Inmates backed up several feet and we pushed the gate partially inward. I stepped into the opening. The inmates were standing motionless, with no movement. I looked at the inmate directly in front of me and he looked down at me. When I saw the slight smirk appear on his face, I could read his mind. He was thinking – no way could this little guy stop me from coming out. He knew that he could toss me like a basketball – but he wouldn't do that. Just then I felt two bodies brush behind me as they were exiting the cell block. I then knew that whoever had been under attack, had now exited. Very slowly I backed out of the cell block and slammed the gate.

We had two cell blocks engulfed in a riot. I had a decision to make. *Were the rest of the five additional cell blocks going to riot? Were my twenty officers in harms away?* I decided that they were in harms away and I had to get them out fast. Quietly, we passed the word to the COs in the remaining blocks to come to the front calmly and get out of the block. We didn't know if every block was involved, but we needed to get the men out if we could. We would lock up the blocks to keep the prisoners in, but we didn't want any more hostages. We'd been able to get some of our COs out of block five and block seven. But we didn't have them all. The inmates had five, and they had demands they wanted met before they would let our men go free.

Several of the inmates in the cell block got my attention. They told me that they weren't going to take part in the riot and they would lock into their cells. *I had to decide – was I going to risk the safety of two officers to try and lock them in – no way.* **I commanded one of my officers to give the cell block keys to one inmate. That inmate opened up the panel boxes for all of those cells within the cell block number two area. All of the inmates locked in without any trouble**

That's where the adult inmates who rioted in 1975 were smarter than the adolescents who had taken me hostage three years before. The adults had a plan; the adolescents had only anger. The adolescents wanted concessions from the warden and thought that taking me, whom the warden held in high regard, would be enough to bring change. But wardens can only change so much. They have limited resources, and they take orders from above. The adults knew that change had to come from higher up. They knew that Judge Lasker didn't like things at Rikers much better than they did, and that he might have the power to make it change. So that's who they asked to see. They wanted to sit down with the judge, the district attorney, and the chairman of the State Board of Corrections and deliver their grievances face to face.

One by one, the authorities came to the jail, and the officers prepared themselves for a fight. Deputy Warden Harris and Warden Graziano came first. We mobilized reinforcements in case we had to use force. We summoned off-duty officers from our regular roster. Headquarters sent officers from other institutions. Men came in from the other facilities on the island, and a backup of police officers was also on hand in full riot gear. We briefly used tear gas in one of the cellblocks. The one casualty from the tear gas was actually Warden Graziano, who was burned when a canister of gas blew up in his hand.

Then the judge, Correction Board Chairman Peter Tufo, Correction Commissioner Bernard Malcolm, DA Mario Merola, and Herman Schwartz from the State Board of Corrections came to negotiate. It was a long night that ran into the next day, but by afternoon, they cut a deal. The hostages were released, and the city got back control of its jail. The deal was put in writing, the inmates were given amnesty, and the Department of Corrections promised to address the prisoners' grievances. Some of the grievances even got addressed, at least in the short term.

THE CITY OF NEW YORK
DEPARTMENT OF CORRECTION
N.Y.C. House of Detention for Men
14-14 Hazen Street
East Elmhurst, N.Y. 11370

BENJAMIN J. MALCOLM
Commissioner

JAMES A. THOMAS
Warden

Tel. 274-2400

AGREEMENT

1. The District Attorney of Bronx County, who has jurisdiction of Rikers Island, agrees that if all of the five Correction Officers are returned in good health, all inmates lock in, that there will be no criminal charge pressed for actions which resulted in property destruction or holding of the five Correction Officers.

2. The Commissioner of the Department of Correction agrees that there shall not be any administrative acations taken against inmates for the event beginning at 9:30 PM, November 23, 1975 through November 24, 1975, nor shall there be any retaliation on any inmates as a result of the activities during this period.

3. That there shall be implemented immediately a special review board to monitor the New York City House of Detention for Men so that no punitive actions will be undertaken by correctional personnel and which shall review and attempt to solve, along with interested and institutional personnel, any grievances which will be brought to their attention. The committee shall consist of two members of the New York City Board of Correction and one member from the New York City Department of Correction.

3A. SEE ATTACHED SHEETS

4. That the Commissioner and the department shall address the following problems with all the resources at their command:
   a) Overcrowding.
   b) The Bail System
   c) Continued due process in inmate institutional disciplinary procedures.
   d) That during visiting there will be no obstruction or harassment of visitors.
   e) Improved medical care, and all other programs designed for the well being of the inmates population.

5. None of the negotiating committee shall be transferred except by voluntary request or sentence. The committee is composed of those names noted on the attached listing.

6. The news media shall be admitted periodically to ascertain the progress noted in this agreement.

SIGNED ON NOVEMBER 24, 1975 BY THE FOLLOWING:

Post Riot Agreement Between Inmates and Commissioner,
Bronx DA & NYS Correction Board

The department made arrangements to transfer the responsibility for medical care from city employees to the private Montefiore Hospital. That meant more resources, better paid medical staff, and presumably better care. A special court was set up at Rikers to review bail, and in about a quarter of the cases it heard, bail was reduced so that some of the men could get out while waiting for their trials. The department tried to deal with overcrowding by transferring some prisons to a detention facility in Brooklyn. Those were short-term adjustments, not fundamental changes to the system. Today, things on Rikers Island are apparently as bad as ever, or worse. By acting up, the prisoners got a bit of relief. But it never should take a riot—not if we run the jails the right way.

N.Y. Daily News Article November 25. 1975

CHAPTER 19

Time for Roy to Go

I was thankful to get through that riot without any injuries and with my men safe with their own families. However, I didn't realize as I sat down to carve the turkey that Thanksgiving that my own time at Rikers was coming to an end.

For whatever reason, and it still mystifies me, Warden Graziano didn't seem to want me around. Even though I was one of his most senior officers, he never took the time to talk to me when he arrived at Rikers in the second half of 1975. He was taking over from Warden Goldstein, who had filled in temporarily after Warden Thomas retired. Coming into a new situation, I would have expected him to talk to all of his veterans to hear from them what was going on at the institution. He might have asked if they had issues that needed his attention or ideas for making things run as smoothly as possible. Even after the riots, when I had been the senior officer on duty, he never asked me my thoughts about what had gone wrong and whether we handled things in the right way. I never knew if he was pleased with my decisions that night or thought I had made any mistakes. Judge Lasker thanked me and even said I'd been a hero. But my direct boss was silent.

I thought it odd, but I could do my job whether I had a close relationship with the warden or none at all. That's what I resolved to do. However, two incidents—one of them puzzling and one of them alarming—convinced me that it was time to call it quits. And if I had any second thoughts, an unusual order from Graziano put them to rest.

The first incident involved another CO, a new captain, Al DeRosa, who refused to follow my orders even though I was his superior officer. I was the duty officer for the institution, which meant I had overall responsibility for everything that happened during my shift. It was my job to monitor the other officers, provide direction when questions came up, and assign the men to set things straight as issues arose.

I had been alerted by the officer in cellblock three that one of his inmates had a problem and he needed some help. I summoned Captain DeRosa, who had responsibility for that block. A medium-sized but rough-looking character of about five feet ten, the guy looked like a prizefighter whose face had been on the receiving end of too many blows. He strode with a bit of a strut, kind of like a cowboy ready for any battles that came his way.

I said to the man, "Captain, we've got an inmate with a problem. I'd like you to look into it." He was brusque: "I don't handle inmate problems," he declared. He turned his back and walked off.

I was shocked. I'd never faced that sort of direct defiance nor witnessed it in more than twenty years as a CO. And if the man didn't handle inmate problems, what exactly did he do? Handling inmate problems is exactly what a CO does.

DeRosa had to come back around on his tour. I decided to wait until he made it back to cellblock three, so I could give him a second chance. Otherwise, I would have to put him on report, something I typically tried to avoid. I also figured I should have a witness in case Captain DeRosa declined to do his job again, so I told the cellblock CO to stay by my side.

History repeated itself. In fact, I could barely get the words out of my mouth when DeRosa cut me off sharply: "I told you, I don't handle inmate problems," he said more emphatically than the first time. I gave him a new command: "Captain, I want to see you in the warden's office." But he ignored me again, walking off on his rounds. I asked the officer in the block to write a report of what he'd just seen, including Captain DeRosa's refusal to obey direct orders from a ranking officer.

Then, things got even crazier. I'd stopped in the control room to talk to the new shift commander, an ADW named Bill. He was a big guy but gentle. Bill was always ready to help another officer or an inmate. If an inmate needed help, Bill would follow up to see that things were taken care of, if there was anything we could do.

While I was talking to Bill, DeRosa stormed in. He wasn't satisfied to defy me; he seemed to want a fistfight as well. DeRosa shouted at me, hollering like a crazy man and walking quickly straight at me. I had to make a choice, to find out what was in his head. I could assume it was a fight and hit him first, or stand there and let him hit me. Getting hit first was going to hurt, if that was what DeRosa wanted. But it also would make clear who started what. Striking first on my part would make it just a fight between two officers, and it would look equally bad for the both of us.

I stood my ground and didn't move. It took all my willpower, but I held my hands clasped in front of me, just below my belt buckle. I was determined not to raise my arms, not even in defense. DeRosa stopped inches from me, so close I could feel his breath. I heard it, too. He pulled back his right arm as far as he could, tempting me to respond. But it was a deliberately telegraphed blow, not the short, quick swat he would throw if he really planned to hit me. He was baiting me, daring me to swing. But hitting me first was a line he didn't seem to want to cross. His behavior told me he wasn't crazy, that his defiance was all planned in his head.

Eyeball to eyeball, we glared at each other. "Captain," I said, "I want a report on your actions, including your refusal to obey an order from a superior officer." Once again, DeRosa stormed away.

I turned to Bill and asked for a report of what he'd seen.

The next day, Bill came to me with report in hand. "Roy," he said, "I want you to know that guy DeRosa came to me after you left. 'Don't give that SOB a report,' he told me. 'We're both Paisanos, and Paisanos stick together.' I didn't answer him then, Roy. But here's that report."

DeRosa went up on charges and conceded his guilt. We didn't cross paths more than necessary after that. I couldn't imagine why he thought he could be so defiant, but the comment about Paisanos got me thinking. The new warden was Italian, too, and DeRosa had come with him at Warden Graziano's request. I wondered if DeRosa thought that some form of ethnic solidarity gave him liberty to do as he pleased. Was there some kind of understanding between the warden and this new captain, who had worked together before?

I didn't want to think that was possible. In two decades serving half a dozen wardens, I'd always been treated fairly. Even when I was one of the few black officers, I never felt disrespected by the man at the top. I hoped that would continue to be the case, but DeRosa's actions, his remark about Paisanos, and his ties to the new warden signaled that things might be changing. It was one more reason to be alert.

A few weeks later came a second incident that was equally unprecedented. This event was even more unsettling because it suggested that my physical safety was at risk. I had always accepted the normal risks of the job because I felt that the forces of the institution stood behind me. I knew that inmates generally would avoid direct threats or life-threatening assaults because they didn't want to risk the consequences. Institutional power helped keep me and other COs safe. But in March 1976, my confidence in that invisible but real shield was taken away.

On this day, I was called to the control room, one of the most crucial areas in the jail. If an officer needed assistance or a response team was required to address a problem, it was handled by the control room. The control room was always manned by a correctional officer under the direction of a captain.

I didn't know why I'd been called to the control room. That was unusual, though not troubling by itself. After all, it was usually a safe place for an officer to be. But what happened after that was an alarm flashing in my face. I walked down the corridor and through the rotunda, an open area that connected to the various cellblocks and could be watched from the control room.

When I arrived, there were three sentenced inmates nearby. They were wearing the telltale green uniforms of men who have been convicted of some offense. Although Rikers was a detention center at that time, there were always a handful of sentenced inmates around because they'd been given jobs to keep the jail running or because they were waiting to be transferred upstate. So it wasn't odd to see a sentenced inmate at Rikers. But it was very unusual to see three of them unsupervised and hanging out outside the control room. Prisoners might walk through that area on their way somewhere else, but they rarely lingered. And when I did run into inmates there, I could count on a nod or friendly acknowledgement, even a smile. These guys and this day were different.

They were cold and remote, standing in a tight huddle clearly closed to anyone else. From their body language and the way they held their shoulders and backs in relation to me, I sensed they were talking about me.

I didn't know these men or think they knew me. I wondered if my mind was playing games. I needed to find out by making very deliberate but obvious movements to see if they responded in some way.

Still in plain view of the control room station, I changed my position, walking slowly away from where they stood. But the nearness of the control room didn't offer the usual comfort because, oddly, there was no officer visible there. I headed toward a small desk, circled around, and pulled up a seat as if I had important paperwork to do.

They moved, too.

In unison, the three of them broke their huddle and walked slowly toward me. I could feel their vibe, and it was hostile, hostile, hostile. They circled behind the desk.

I was seated in the middle of three chairs. The shortest inmate pulled out the chair on my right and settled in beside me. Silently, he looked into my eyes with a cold, threatening gaze. A second inmate seated himself just as silently to my left. This was *not* what inmates do with COs. The tallest one took a position directly behind me. I was boxed in. I saw it, I felt it, I knew it. I was surrounded. **I was their prey.**

The one to my right was in charge. **Slowly, he put both feet up on the desk, with insolence. It was a dare.** His eyes said to me, "I have sat at your desk. I have propped up my feet, and I am looking right at you. Do you have anything to say?"

I stared back directly into his eyes. But that was as much as I was going to do. There were three of them. I wasn't stupid. I wasn't going to start a brawl.

He tried another taunt. Slowly, he took his feet down from the desk. Still looking at me, he opened the desk drawer. An inmate opening a deputy warden's desk drawer? That DOES NOT happen. But that's what he did. All the time, his eyes were in my face as if to say, "I dare you to object. Go ahead, say something, tell me you don't like it." He challenged me in silence.

I said nothing. But my eyes burrowed back into his. He could read me, and I could read him. I was not going to do anything crazy. But I also wasn't going to be intimidated. He closed that drawer slowly and opened the one below. He glanced down for a moment to see what he might find there. Then his eyes came back to me, resuming the dare.

I decided to change the dynamic. I knew that if I got back on my feet, I'd be in a better position to challenge them. I didn't know how far they would go. Would they grab me? Choke me? Stab me? But I decided to find out. Very slowly, I raised myself up. I took my eyes off them, knowing that they would communicate with each other and decide their next move. They had hoped to intimidate me and instill fear. Instead, they made me angry. I rose slowly from my chair, and with each inch I felt more confident, ready for whatever they might do. They would make a decision—or the leader would—and I would find out.

Then I was up. As I rose, two of them moved as well – repositioning themselves while they waited to see what I would do. Slowly, I turned to my left and two inmates were now standing where I chose to walk. I strode straight toward them. If they wanted to fight, I would do it.

As I came toward them, I saw movement. From their eyes and body language, I sensed they'd decided against a fistfight with a deputy warden. They visibly backed up, shuffling their feet to clear a path and let me know they weren't going to fight.

Their faces showed surprise and a bit of respect that I hadn't been cowed. With each step forward by me and backward by them, my confidence swelled. I had become the challenger instead of the challenged. I knew that these three guys would never again be enlisted against me.

But I also knew there might be others. As I walked past them, I thought of the bigger problem I faced. Only one person had the power to create this scenario, shutting down the control room area and keeping it clear except for me and inmates who threatened me. These inmates had felt immune, knowing that I would not get help from the control room. I knew that I could never be safe anywhere in this institution. This would have to be my last day in the Department of Corrections. I had become prey.

To me, the message was clear. I could be dead at any moment. Perhaps the only intent was intimidation. They had tested how I would react. It was like they wanted to be sure what they were getting into before they made a move.

After twenty-one years, I was confident I could read inmates, their body language, and what was inside their heads. I could have been reading these inmates wrong. But I didn't think so then, and I don't think so now.

I felt a chill in my bones, a sense of danger I had never felt before in twenty-one years wearing the badge. It was clear I could be harassed by inmates with no fear. In my mind, I was a dead man walking. I couldn't do my job with that feeling hanging over me. So close after DeRosa's defiance, I saw a pattern that would never let me be comfortable at Rikers again.

It was time to leave. Right then, no waiting. Warden Graziano reinforced my decision. After months of ignoring me, he summoned me—*that same day*. He called me into his office, and with barely a word of greeting, he brusquely ordered me to post some new regulations that the department had just issued. That was odd, as it was not usually an assignment for a senior officer. But I assured him I would have them posted immediately.

But that wasn't good enough. "No," he clarified. "Don't have somebody else post them. I want YOU to do it—throughout the building. And if any of them come down, I expect you to personally put them back up. I will hold you responsible." It was fraternity-level hazing, an assignment for a junior officer or even an inmate clerk. It was a strange order to give a ranking officer who was supposed to be overseeing the entire jail during that shift. To me, it was another message: a deliberate insult to let me know that I was his target, and he would harass me until I was gone.

After more than two decades of trying to do the right thing even when others doubted me or scoffed, it was time to go. I headed straight to headquarters to file my retirement papers. I was going to walk out of Rikers on my own, alive, and as soon as possible. Then there was one final stunner. At headquarters, I learned from a friend that Warden Graziano had been a step ahead. He had called to find out if I had enough service time to retire. He hadn't wanted me to leave until he got his licks in. That's how it looked to me.

Perhaps he didn't like what he'd heard about me and the way I dealt with inmates. Thomas had given me carte blanche, supporting my belief that helping inmates was the point of my job. Maybe Graziano didn't see it that way. Maybe he just didn't want any Thomas men around. I read his intentions, but I couldn't read his mind. My life was going to be hell if I stayed. Returning to the institution to pack up my things, I was told that the warden wanted to see me. Twice in one day he wanted to see me? He had been there for months and had never spoken to me once. I walked in and his demeanor had changed. He was conciliatory, or pretended to be, and asked in a polite voice, "Deputy Caldwood, what can I give you so that you won't retire?"

"Warden," I said, "there's nothing you can do for me. I want nothing. I'm gone." Then I turned, showing him my back, and walked away.

CHAPTER 20

In Conclusion

There were a few more acts. I kept my hand in, thinking I could still make things a bit better for my former colleagues and the inmates I'd left behind.

At the time I left Rikers, I had been working to bring in the Black Rodeo to entertain the inmates, and I wanted to make that happen even after I retired. It took about seventy permits from the city, but we got it done. Cowboys and bronco busters and nearly one hundred animals came over the bridge to Rikers from downtown New York. They showed the inmates how to ride bulls, rope calves, and get horses to jump over barrels. Most of the inmates had grown up watching western movies and TV shows, but they were all from New York City and not many had seen horses and bulls and cowboys in real life. They loved it, whooping and clapping. Some rooted for the cowboys and some rooted for the bulls, but they all had a good time. At the end, we had a small glitch. Some of the cowboys had forgotten their IDs, and we had to negotiate to get them *off* the island when the show was done. IDs are necessary to show that you're not an inmate trying to sneak away.

It was such a success that I volunteered to put together another program that would give the inmates a chance to ride horses. The Department of Corrections agreed I could bring back some horses and a few instructors from the Black Rodeo. The rodeo gave us some Black Rodeo kerchiefs as well as some free cigarettes to distribute. Some young women dressed up as cowgirls to distribute the kerchiefs and the smokes.

But the security was lax. There was some kind of miscommunication, so we had inmates out in a field without any COs around. I had to keep the girls and the riders on the bus until I tracked down a captain I had worked with to round up some security. In the end, we made it happen, but the lapse suggested it might not be safe to do it again. I haven't been back to Rikers since.

Still, I didn't completely turn my back. In 1980, four years after I had retired, there was a move by the state to take over Rikers Island and begin using it to house state prisoners. The mayor, the governor, the state commissioner, and the city commissioner of correction were all in favor of the sale. As a neighbor and former officer, I thought it was a bad idea. I worked with our citizens' association to fight the state's bid, participated in every public discussion on the subject, and spoke up at several hearings. In the end, the three commissioners who had the final say on this matter agreed with us in saying no to the state. I liked to think I helped turn the tide.

I also stayed interested in the young men inside. To this day, thirty-eight years later, I volunteer at the Addicts Rehabilitation Center in Harlem, which works with former inmates to help them rebuild their lives after time behind bars. Being back in that arena and having another chance to help these young men is extremely rewarding. One time, I traveled to Albany with ARC director Jim Allen for two days of meetings with members of the state assembly to tell them about our work. I shared a hotel room with one of the ARC officers that night, and it turned out he had been an inmate in cellblock seven at Rikers when I was taken hostage. That was a bizarre coincidence that threw me off stride for a few minutes. But we wound up having a good discussion about Rikers and how to give prisoners a helping hand both in jail and afterward. I was delighted to see that this man had survived his time in custody and had been able to build a good life for himself. During my retirement, the city of New York also made right on one of the disappointments of my career, belatedly awarding a medal that I was supposed to receive almost three decades before. In 1972, I was among several dozen officers invited with our families to travel to city hall and receive commendations. I was slated to get a medal for my actions when I was taken hostage and also for the Steam Table Incident. I planned to give the medal to my grandson, and I was full of anticipation as other officers received their medals. When the man next to me let me look at his medal, my heart quickened a bit more as I thought what it would mean to my grandson.

NYC Dept. of Corrections Award Ceremony

My name was called, and I went up front for handshakes and kind words, but when I opened the box to look at my medal, there was nothing there. I'd been given an empty box! I was assured I would get a medal later. But almost thirty years later, it still hadn't shown up. Out of the blue, in 2001, I received a call from Mayor Giuliani's office and was invited to a special awards ceremony. Apparently some old colleagues had been lobbying on my behalf, and the mayor wanted to correct the mistake. It was never my goal to win medals. But I confess the empty box had grated on me, and it made me feel damn good when Mayor Giuliani and other city officials presented me with a Bravery Recognition plaque.

Roy receiving his Bravery Recognition award in 2001
(pictured with Chief of the Department Bob Daveron)

Looking back, I am comfortable that I conducted myself well during my career and was true to my responsibilities to provide good care to the inmates. Naturally, I made my share of mistakes, but by and large I am confident that I made more good decisions than bad. I feel good about the weddings and the other ways I made jail a little better. Among my possessions, I treasure a note from a former inmate who went from Rikers to do time upstate but still wanted to console me after I was taken hostage:

"Dear Captain Caldwood, in my eyes you have always been a beautiful black brother and father to me and the other kids on the rocks. Listen, Captain Caldwood, I know you are a good man, please don't change your ways because of what happened in seven-block."

That made me feel good.

Of course, I have some regrets. In twenty-one years, you are going to make some mistakes.

I had deliberately avoided learning too much about any inmate. I wanted to have a clean slate in my mind so that I could treat them fairly and equally. But in some instances, I regret keeping that distance. I wish I had found out more about a few of them. I wonder now what happened to the Big Bear and whether I could have made a long-term difference in his life had I tried to change the way others treated him. I don't know which young inmate pulled me to safety out of the tear gas barrage when I was a hostage. I've always believed that action saved my life. I wish I had tried to find out who he was just to say thanks. Maybe I could have helped him after he got out of jail. I might have kept up with Cuba, the leader of the 1972 revolts who had mostly acted with restraint and common sense. In 2013, forty years after I'd last seen him, Cuba was found dead on a golf course where he foraged for golf balls and sold them to earn a few dollars.

He had been stabbed sixteen times. I read about it in the newspaper and wondered how it had come to that.

But the thing that troubles me most is that as bad as it was when I retired, Rikers Island appears to be an even worse place to be today.

Newspapers don't tell the whole story. Nobody really knows what it's like inside Rikers or any other jail unless they've lived it. But the stream of reports of needless deaths, neglect, and violence makes clear that things are not good.

In August 2014, the US attorney for Manhattan, Preet Bharara, found a "deep-seated culture of violence" against adolescent inmates at Rikers. His report said more than four out of every ten young inmates were victims of CO violence at least once. "It is a place where brute force is the first impulse rather than the last resort, a place where verbal insults are repaid with physical injuries, where beatings are routine while accountability is rare," Bharara said.[42]

The New York Times, in reports of its own, uncovered a general surge of violence at all of the ten facilities now operating at Rikers. It said the use of force by COs had more than doubled over ten years. It also pointed out that inmate attacks on officers and other inmates had gone up for five years in a row.[43] A jump in the number of mentally ill inmates, who are more aggressive and can't control themselves very well, may be partly to blame. In 2014, about 40 percent of Rikers inmates had mental health problems, and they accounted for about two-thirds of all rules violations.

---

42 "US Inquiry Finds a 'Culture of Violence' against Teenage Inmates at Rikers," *The New York Times*, August 4, 2014.

43 "Rikers Island Struggles with Surge in Violence and Mental Illness," *The New York Times*, March 18, 2004, and "Rikers: Where Mental Illness Meets Brutality in Jail," July 14, 2014.

But from my experience, the fundamental problem is poor leadership from the top of the Department of Corrections. When I was a CO, Commissioner Anna Kross repeatedly reminded us that everything we did should help the inmates. It wasn't our job to punish them further. And she also reminded us that in the case of detainees, they were innocent until proven guilty.

New York City's new mayor, William de Blasio, who took office in 2014, and his new correctional commissioner, Joseph Ponte, have promised to clean it up. It is my belief that Mayor de Blasio really cares and is concerned about all of the communities in New York City—including those of color. He is truly trying to find solutions for all of his inherited problems. Ponte, who did a lot of good reform work in Maine's jails before coming to New York, has said that one way to cut violence is to treat prisoners humanely. "If we can enlist their cooperation through positive reinforcement, why not do that?" he says.[44] That's the sort of approach I tried to practice in my own way when I was at Rikers.

But that kind of caregiving approach doesn't come naturally to everybody. Many of the COs I served with believed that inmates deserved whatever hardship that came their way. Many still think that way. In Maine, some jail officers made fun of Ponte's ideas as "Hug a Thug." Norman Seabrook, the head of New York City's CO union, worries that inmates get off too easy for assaulting officers and other violations. In Maine, Ponte gave aged inmates one-hour "time-outs" for some types of infractions. Seabrook says, "A time-out is what you give your grandchildren."[45]

Sadly, the relationship today between the police department and many citizens is unnecessarily toxic. People of color, in particular, are unduly targeted by too many young officers and wind up behind bars without

---

44 "The Prison Reformer vs. Rikers Island," *The New York Times*, April 4, 2014.
45 Ibid, *The New York Times*, p. 104.

good cause. But it takes guts for officers to reach out to the community and build positive connections when colleagues think they've gone soft headed.

Doing the right thing can be hard, but when you give respect, you get respect. Positive actions can produce positive reactions. If an officer shows he cares, the community will help. After all, most people in every community want a safe environment. They will help the police officers they trust.

Actions speak louder than words. It's not about making just any move. It's about making the right moves, which sometimes means going against the grain instead of going along. Do enough law enforcement officers—and their bosses—have the guts to make the right moves today?

We need a conversation *with* people of all colors and races and not *at* them or *about* them. Until minorities have a seat at the table and help make the policies that affect their everyday lives, we will not have justice or peace. If we want to fix the problems in the jails, we need to fix the problems outside the jails as well.

One thing I know for sure is that many of today's problems are the same ones that I saw forty years ago. Too often, we put people in jails and prisons because we don't know what else to do with them (or when we do know, we don't want to spend the money to do something different).

We are continuing to fill the jails with inconvenient people: the poor, the uneducated, the mentally ill, drug addicts, and alcoholics. These days, the prisoners are almost always black or Hispanic. Very few white people wind up behind bars. Very few rich people serve time either.

Yes, violent criminals belong in prison. Nobody wants murders or rapists walking the street. Nobody wants to worry about getting mugged when they leave their house. Big-time drug dealers also should do time. White-collar criminals should be punished, too. Deliberately hurting others or stealing their money is just cause for punishment whether you do it with a gun or an accounting trick.

But addicts, alcoholics, and the mentally ill need help, not jail. Petty street hustlers and scammers need jobs and a chance to earn a living honestly. Voters in California took a step in that direction in November 2014 when they approved a measure to convert some lesser crimes from felonies to misdemeanors.[46] That will mean shorter sentences and less time behind bars for thousands who do not pose a significant threat to public safety. Our country would be better off if we could give more petty criminals the helping hand and support they need to make an honest living and live by the law. I have to believe we can use some of the energy that invents new technologies or finds new ways to get rich to identify productive alternatives to jail.

Nobody should ever spend time in jail because they are too poor to pay bail. "Innocent until proven guilty" means that people generally shouldn't be doing time in some jail while waiting for trial. Perhaps we should compensate people for lost wages if they've spent time in jail and are later acquitted—something to make up for the mistake and disruption to their lives.

Pretrial detention should be rare—only to keep truly dangerous people off the street. But grounds for such detention should be carefully thought out. We need smart lawyers, judges, police officers, psychologists, and social workers to figure out how to do it.

And when people are found guilty, we ought to be smart about the sentences. Some should go to rehab centers; others could do community service. Some could be told to put their talents (or money) to work for drug

---

46 *The Los Angeles Times*, "Prop. 47 passes, reducing some criminal penalties," by Paige St. John, November 4, 2014, http://www.latimes.com/local/political/la-me-ff-prop-47-drug-possession-20141103-story.html.

rehab or sentenced to community service. When you've made one mistake, obeyed the law for years, and are working productively, we should think very hard before putting you behind bars. There has to be a better way to make people who've corrected themselves "pay" for old crimes.

By putting the right people in prisons and jails, we will go a long way toward making the jails better and reducing violence. Put the mentally ill and addicts in a place where they can get help, and we will reduce much of the tension and strains that now lead to fights and outright brutality. Doing so also would reduce overcrowding—the other great source of tension and danger in jail. We need to have the right balance between correctional officers and inmates. That means fewer inmates and more officers. When I was at Rikers, we often had a single man patrolling 150 inmates or more in an area almost as long as a football field. How can one person be expected to do that, and do it well?

We need better systems to help prisoners when they are released back into society. If you went into jail or prison without the education, training, or community ties to make an honest living, you probably have less of a chance when you get out. **Putting people behind bars is the easy part. The harder work of helping them stay straight should be at the top of an American to-do list.** I am encouraged by the so-called "ban-the-box" movement, which would give former inmates a better chance to find jobs by removing questions about criminal records from job applications. Employers would still be able to run individual background checks on qualified employees, but they wouldn't be able to arbitrarily eliminate every applicant who had a mistake at some point in his or her life. Depending on the job responsibility, some former inmates probably should not be hired because of their records, but we should do what we can to give them a fair chance.[47]

---

47 National Employment Law Project: www.nelp.org/banthebox.

Finally, we must do a better job of training correctional officers, teaching them how to deal with mentally ill and other troubled inmates without resorting to violence first. We need to teach COs to think of themselves as caregivers who treat prisoners with respect. We must give COs the resources they need to make the right moves in tough situations. We need to build modern facilities and create jails that are as safe and well run as possible. And we also must give COs the respect they deserve for doing a tough and stressful job that helps keep the rest of us safe but that very few of us are willing to do.

Acknowledgments

Editor: Michael Gelb
Co-developer: Diane Royer
Cover Photography: Magnet4

I would like to acknowledge my family for encouraging me and supporting my efforts to write this book: my wife, Muriel Caldwood; my daughters, Karen Caldwood and Diane Royer; my grandchildren, Yvonne Tejada, Terrence Royer, Christopher Royer, and Racquel Royer; my cousin Frank Ross; and my grandnephew Anthony White.

I would also like to thank:

Anna Kross (NYC Dept. of Correction commissioner 1954–1965), a bold, visionary woman who was responsible for the most dynamic changes in the history of correction. Her motto was: "Whatever you do must be to help the inmates." I will never forget those words of advice.

Benjamin Malcolm (NYC Dept. of Correction commissioner 1972–1977), for these words to me: "Your excellent work as program planner and consultant to the academy is the kind of team effort we are striving to create."

Federal Judge Morris Lasker, who was present during the 1975 riot and the postriot negotiation meeting, where he acknowledged me with the kind words, "You are a true hero."

Dr. Vincent Dole, who developed methadone maintenance therapy. I am privileged to have known him and observed his dedication to treating inmates with heroin addiction.

Barbara Margolis, an American prisoner's rights advocate, pioneer, mentor, unsung heroine, and the "mother" many prison adolescents never had.

Warden James Thomas, became the first appointed African American warden on Rikers Island. His complete faith in me and his support allowed me to create and lead many unprecedented programs at Rikers Island.

Jacqueline McMickens, JD (NYC Dept. of Correction commissioner 1984–1986), a trailblazer and female pioneer in the Department of Correction and a visionary and strong supporter who acknowledged my unique approach and invited me to lecture at the Correction Academy.

Helen Marshall (Queens Borough president 2001–2013), a true grassroots leader, my neighbor, my friend, and my supporter.

Dr. George Blair (former SUNY vice chancellor and president of the Ascent Foundation), a transformational leader who inspired me to never be satisfied, but to push on and to always follow my dreams.

James Allen (founder and executive director emeritus of the Addicts Rehabilitation Center – ARC) a pioneer, friend, and unsung hero who touched so many lives through his compassion to help those with drug addiction and former inmates who wanted another chance in life.

Ronald Taylor (retired sergeant of the New York State Dept. of Correction), a role model, dedicated correctional officer, and family friend whom I mentored. His work approach embodied many of my principles.

The unseen and unknown adolescent who risked his life to save me from friendly fire.

I'd also like to give acknowledgment and appreciation to the many thousands of both adolescent and adult detainees who proved that humane treatment can produce better human beings.

Author Bio

A former World War II US Army "buffalo soldier" Roy J. Caldwood served in the 92nd Infantry Division before spending over twenty-one years (1955-1976) maintaining calm and order in New York City's prison system.

Starting as a raw recruit, Caldwood rose to the rank of assistant deputy warden on Rikers Island, honing and perfecting a caring, humanistic style that other officers, wardens, and commissioners eventually embraced as the most effective way to treat inmates.

In the words of former Commissioner Jackie McMickens, Caldwood tried to make jail "more livable" for inmates with a combination of respect and smooth institutional operations. Caldwood shared his methods with officer candidates as a lecturer at the Correction Officers Training Academy.

Caldwood's respectful treatment of inmates helped him safely negotiate non-violent solutions to hostage takings, including his own time as a hostage during the 1972 Rikers Island Riot.

In 2001, Caldwood was awarded the Commissioner's Award for Bravery.

Special Tribute

James A. Thomas
Former NYC Dept. of Correction Warden

The late Warden James Thomas was a mentor, role model and friend to me.

I also greatly appreciate the many correction officers who not only survived the most difficult days on Rikers Island but also showed what they were made of. It would be an understatement to just say that they were bold. My fellow officers demonstrated courage, allegiance and fortitude - in the face of danger. Even when they knew a riot was imminent, they took their posts - unarmed in the midst of hundreds of angry inmates. We had each other's back. They set the bar high for the future correction officers.